Dinghy Fishing

MARINER
SEAHOG
HUNTER

Dinghy Fishing

Dave Lewis

Illustrations by Anne Maclean

BLANDFORD

Dedication

My first book on boat fishing is dedicated to my parents and in particular my late father, Fred Lewis, a master mariner and Bristol Channel pilot, from whom I undoubtedly inherited a love of the sea. If it had not been for their constant encouragement during my childhood, when I first showed an interest in angling, and later when I left home at 16 to start my own career at sea, I dare say I would be wasting my time on a golf course or in the garden today!

A BLANDFORD BOOK

First published in the UK 1996 by Blandford,
A Cassell Imprint
Cassell Plc, Wellington House, 125 Strand, London WC2R 0BB

Distributed in the United States by Sterling Publishing Co., Inc.
387 Park Avenue South, New York, NY 10016–8810

Distributed in Australia by Capricorn Link (Australia) Pty Ltd
2/13 Carrington Road, Castle Hill, NSW 2154

British Library Cataloguing-in-Publication Data
A catalogue entry for this title is available from the British Library

ISBN 0–7137–2537–0

Printed and bound in Great Britain by
Hillman Printers (Frome) Ltd

Cover
Jeff Thomas holds his first-ever bass, a wonderful fish weighing 10 lb 4 oz. The fish was caught when fishing an inshore mark with the author.

Title page
Fishing at anchor, both uptide and downtide rods in use

Contents

Foreword

Some time ago I returned from the United States after a 20-year stint on a big circulation sports magazine which had given me the freedom virtually to travel the world and fish where I pleased.

When I came home, however, I was disappointed to find that the shore fishing that I had known before I went away had more or less collapsed, leaving anglers to fish – intentionally, for heaven's sake – for dogfish and tiny pouting . . .

Then I met Dave Lewis – and his dinghy. Dinghy fishing was something that I'd rarely tried around the British Isles – either I had cast or I had gone off-shore in bigger craft. But Dave soon proved to me that fishing out of a dinghy, inshore, was a perfect happy medium.

To start with, it gives the sea fisherman or woman great versatility, greater freedom. Even though the sport may have taken a downturn in local waters, Dave could always hitch up his small craft to a station wagon and head off – to the Orkneys if necessary, or just 20 miles down the coast.

I could tell you many a tale – about the day in the Bristol Channel, for instance, when Dave and I hauled out cod after winter cod, which turned out to be the most delicious I'd ever sampled. No wonder – as we found, when we cleaned them up, that they were stuffed to the gills with prawns!

In the meantime, read and enjoy the words of a genuine expert, a consummate fisherman. And if you end up with your own 16-footer, as I did, I wouldn't be at all surprised.

Clive Gammon

The author holds a trigger fish, caught from a mark that all but dries out at low water.

1 Buying a boat

Buying a boat is a large financial investment, usually the culmination of months or even years of hard saving. Obviously, you will need to buy a boat that is suited to the style of fishing in your area and, if buying second-hand, in good repair.

As far as the choice of materials is concerned, there is little point in considering boats built of anything other than GRP (glass-reinforced plastic, or fibreglass). GRP is extremely strong, easy to maintain and repair and easily the best all-round material for modern small boat construction.

Wooden dinghies are rarely seen today and when they are they are either very expensive or in a poor state of repair, requiring a lot of specialist and very expensive maintenance. An increasing number of aluminium boats have appeared in recent years. Aluminium produces a very strong yet lightweight hull, with excellent performance when matched with relatively small engines. Aluminium offers certain advantages when the angler is faced with poor launch facilities and has to drag his boat over rough ground to the water's edge, as it is very tough and durable. In general, aluminium boats tend to be more suited for inshore rather than offshore fishing.

You should always know exactly which type of boat you require before you part with any cash. The easiest way is to find out what the locals are using. If, for example, local dinghy anglers concentrate on fishing inshore marks, or perhaps within an estuary, there is little point in wasting money on a high-speed boat. On the other hand, if the best of the fishing is well offshore, over wrecks or reefs, a 10-h.p. plodder will be at best a frustration, at worst even a danger. If you are a novice, the best solution is to try and get a couple of trips afloat with an experienced dinghy angler before you buy your own boat. You might even find you don't like fishing from small boats!

Dealers usually stock the types of boat for which there is the strongest local demand. But this is not always the case and some dealers will stock and push those boats with the highest profit margins. Any new boat will look good in the warmth and bright lights of a dealer's showroom, and viewing a boat in a showroom is certainly not the way to decide which boat to buy. Insist that the dealer or private vendor arranges a water trial. If he or she refuses, look elsewhere.

There are many different designs of boats and hulls (Fig. 1) and a novice dinghy angler will find it more or less impossible to assess a boat's performance, not having the experience to draw a comparison against anything else. If you are inexperienced, take someone with you who has a sound knowledge of small boats, preferably someone with a few years' experience fishing your local patch. Remember, most people are experts when it is not their cash at risk.

It is hard to generalize when highlighting features which make a good angling boat and, in all honesty, the ideal boat does not and probably never will exist. All dinghy anglers must be prepared to compromise somewhere, as there is only a limited amount of scope for design and development in a 16-ft or 17-ft hull. The trick is never to compromise in any way on safety.

Look for a boat with a good freeboard, in layman's terms that is a boat with high sides. Knee height should be considered as the minimum amount of acceptable freeboard. Adding rails will enhance on-board safety and minimize the risk of falling overboard, but they will add nothing towards keeping the water out!

A good angling boat will have a lot of free deck space. Bear in mind that a new and empty hull in a showroom may well look spacious, but what will it be like when kitted out for a day's fishing with petrol tanks, anchor and fish boxes, as well as a couple of anglers with their mountains of fishing tackle? Remember, only flat areas of deck space can be used for walking on when at sea. Boats with curved sides and a relatively small flat deck might look spacious but they can cause real problems on the water, especially when the deck is wet and slippery.

Boats with plenty of dry locker stowage space are easy boats to keep uncluttered. There is nothing worse or more dangerous than fishing from an untidy and cluttered boat. A good amount of stowage room provides safe stowage for all items of equipment. Lockable lockers are not necessarily secure stowage compartments, though they are a deterrent to the opportunist thief.

Look for a sump or bilge built into the deck that will act as a collection point for spray and rain water. This will help to keep the deck dry and will often be the ideal place to install the pick-up tube for a bilge pump or the transducer for a fish finder.

Having decided which boat to buy, it is very important to match it with a suitable engine. Many matched boat/engine packages are now available but, once again, there will always be the dealer who will recommend an engine which will overpower or underpower a boat, simply because that particular engine happens to be in stock.

All boats have a recommended maximum and minimum power range. It is often advisable to try to buy the most powerful engine recommended for use with your boat. Then, when the boat is fully kitted out and with anglers aboard, you can expect the boat to return a reasonable performance. Never be tempted to overpower a boat, the result could be fatal. If in doubt, seek advice from the boat manufacturer.

The trailer is usually the most underestimated and least-considered part of the boat package. The first time many anglers realize that they have bought an unsuitable trailer will usually be the first time they launch and retrieve the boat. Most damage caused to trailered boats

Fig. 1 Cross-sections of hull designs.

Cathedral planing hull

Deep 'V' hull

Semi-displacement hull

Displacement hull

occurs at the launch site, and a high percentage of these accidents are easily prevented by using a decent trailer. For this reason I have included an extensive section on buying trailers.

Buying second-hand

Buying second-hand boats, engines and trailers is just like buying anything else second-hand, and carries a certain amount of risk. Second-hand fishing boat packages are widely advertised in local newspapers and the national angling press. As with anything else, there are a few genuine bargains around if you are prepared to look for them, some that are a reasonable buy, and plenty of rubbish.

If you are inexperienced, it is vital that you take someone with you who knows small boats inside out, even if it means paying for the service. Obviously the advice already given on the choice of a suitable boat is just as relevant when buying second-hand as when buying new. Most of us choose to buy a second-hand package because cash is tight. Having bought the package there will be little cash left to spend on rectifying defects.

Try to buy a hull of a known pedigree from a well-established company. There are many small independent boat builders, many of whom produce excellent products. Unfortunately such excellence is not standard, and I would advise against buying any hull of unknown origin.

Second-hand engines are always a big gamble. If possible, it is sensible to try and buy a second-hand boat and trailer, and then buy a new engine. Any second-hand engine should immediately receive a full and thorough service from a qualified marine mechanic, who has the knowledge, experience and specialist tools to service your engine fully.

Before you actually buy the engine you should get it examined. Explain that you will be prepared to pay for a qualified mechanic to give the engine a good once-over, including service, if the report turns out satisfactory. If, on the other hand, the engine proves to be a dud, the vendor pays the bill.

Whenever buying a second-hand GRP hull, examine it closely for signs of osmosis. Osmosis, in this context, is the term used to describe the delamination of fibreglass due to an ingress of moisture. The fibreglass matting is protected by a high-gloss resin finish, known as the gel coat. This should be intact and free from chips and cracks to prevent water from reaching the fibreglass matting beneath. It is the matting which gives the hull its strength. Should the gel coat become damaged, water will then percolate into the matting and, in severe cases, cause delamination of the fibres. This has obvious consequences regarding the strength and overall integrity of the boat's hull.

It is therefore essential that all damage to the protective gel coat layer is repaired as soon as possible, particularly where the damage has occurred below the waterline. Even in the short term, water that has soaked into the fibreglass matting can cause severe damage during cold conditions as the water expands when it freezes, thus forcing the fibres apart and allowing more water to enter.

Trailers

A lot of new boats are sold as part of a complete package which includes a trailer. The majority of new packages are supplied with trailers that are recommended by the boat builder, but not always!

Problems can occur when a boat is bought from one source and the buyer shops around for the cheapest trailer elsewhere. With very few exceptions no trailer manufacturer is going to admit that his products are unsuitable for your boat. Most will probably claim that a couple of 'simple modifications' will transform it into the ideal trailer for you. Usually those simple modifications boost the cost of the trailer higher than if you had opted for the ideal unit. There is only one way to be sure that a particular trailer is suitable for your boat: contact the boat builder and ask for advice.

The primary function of any boat trailer is to transport the boat safely. In order to achieve this smoothly, and without causing damage to any part of the hull, it must firmly support the hull, cushioning it at all points of contact. Nowhere should any part of your boat's hull be allowed to come into contact with metal.

If the boat has a definite central keel, typical on displacement- and semi-displacement-type hulls, then most manufacturers strongly recommend that the weight of the boat is supported along its keel on a line of centre rollers fitted along the trailer's spine or backbone (Fig. 2) and not along any part of the hull or bilges, as would be the case with side-roller-type trailers.

The purpose of the side supports on a trailer, designed to carry a boat with a keel, is solely to prevent any lateral movement while on the road and to prevent the keel slipping off the centre rollers, not to take any weight. Obviously height adjustment on these side supports is critical.

Many of the faster planing-type hulls can be safely carried on roller-type trailers. Without a doubt, this style of trailer makes launching and retrieving as quick and effortless as possible. I would most strongly advise that you consider paying the extra cost of buying this design of trailer, provided that you are sure it is suitable for your hull.

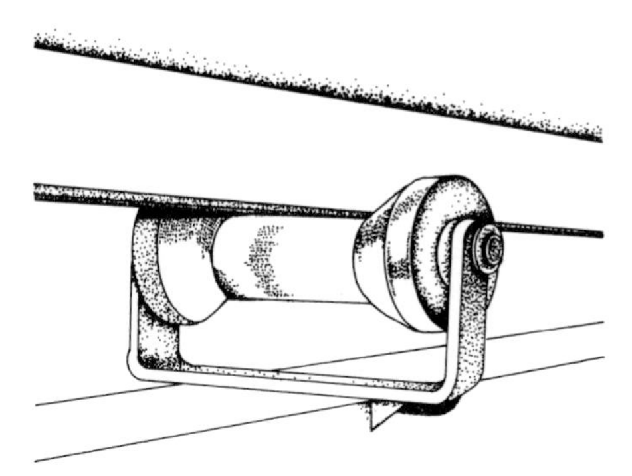

Fig. 2 Keel of boat correctly positioned on a centre roller.

There are other considerations that have to be taken into account when choosing and buying a boat trailer. Avoid any non-galvanized trailers if you intend to use it in a marine environment. It matters little that they may cost considerably less than a galvanized trailer from new. Any immediate cash savings will be eaten up within a very short time with the constant cost and considerable effort of maintaining a non-galvanized trailer against rust. In addition, the resale value of a non-galvanized trailer after a couple of years' use in salt water will be virtually nil.

Some dealers offer the like of jockey wheels as an optional extra, despite the fact that they are essential. With all but the lightest of boats, a jockey wheel is a must, particularly if you launch from a beach. If this is the case you should note that it is often possible to buy a better-quality jockey wheel, at the same or at a lower price, from other suppliers, rather than buying one as an optional extra.

You should always make sure that the trailer is fitted with suspension units rated as being suitable to take the load of the boat, plus anything else that will be stored in it during road transit. Overloaded suspension units will not cushion the hull sufficiently from uneven road surfaces, and this will make towing difficult and possibly damage the hull. The efficient life expectancy of suspension units will be greatly reduced if they are constantly overloaded.

Always check the load capacity of the trailer's winch. The winch takes a lot of strain, and an underpowered winch will not withstand much abuse. The biggest advantage in opting for a more powerful winch is that the reduction in gearing found on heavier-rated models will make the task of winching the boat back on to its trailer a lot easier for you. In addition, the working life expectancy of a powerful winch will be far longer than one straining to work to its maximum limit.

It is good to see that very few trailer manufacturers now supply winches filled with steel cable. A couple of years ago, I narrowly escaped a nasty accident whilst winching my boat back on to its trailer on a flat beach. Totally without warning, the cable snapped, lashing back past my face. The hole made in the firm sand behind left me in no doubt that if I had stood a few inches further to the right, then I would almost certainly have lost an eye. A strong nylon rope makes a much better winch line, and webbing strapping is also very popular, especially with the heaviest trailerable dinghies.

Typical trailer winch loaded with webbing strap, ideal for use with heavy boats.

Whether or not to opt for a double-axle or a braked trailer will depend on the size of your rig and on the law. Two-wheel trailers are fine for boats up to about 15 cwt, but most trailers with carrying capacities greater than this are supplied with four wheels. Four-wheel trailers are considerably heavier so they obviously increase the total load of the rig. It is worth noting that the Caravan Club recommends that the laden weight of the trailer is never more than 85 per cent of the kerb weight of the towing vehicle. Four-wheel trailers offer the additional safety factor of a back-up tyre on each side in the event of a puncture.

All trailers with a design axle weight exceeding 15 cwt must be braked with an EC-approved system, and all braked trailers supplied after 1 April 1989 must also have an auto-reverse system as detailed below. Also, all braked trailers should be fitted with an emergency braking device which will stop the trailer if it becomes detached from the vehicle. A fitted handbrake capable of holding the outfit stationary on an 18 per cent gradient is another legal requirement. Be careful if you buy a trailer imported from the United States. It will probably not conform to EC requirements, and will need an expensive conversion.

In the UK, all braked trailers manufactured since October 1982 must have hydraulically dampened overrun couplings. These activate the trailer brakes automatically and by the appropriate amount, as the towing vehicle is slowed down by its own brakes. In the standard version the brake has to be disconnected when you want to reverse but, as you will have noted, trailers built after 1989 must be fitted with an auto-reverse system which allows the trailer to be reversed by the towing vehicle without the need for disconnection.

Some trailers are designed to assist launch and recovery still further with a break-back, or hinged main frame. This modification allows the whole back part of the trailer to be tilted, greatly assisting launching from a flat beach. A more recent development is the provision of a cross member at the back of the trailer holding a cradle or group of rollers, which tilts in such a way that the rollers support the bow of the boat as it slides off, or as it is brought back on to the trailer. This is another excellent consideration for anyone who launches and retrieves their boat on a regular basis.

DIY trailers

An option for those wishing to keep costs to an absolute minimum is to buy a trailer in kit form and assemble it themselves. Several companies now supply boat trailers for DIY assembly and in most cases a very definite cash saving can be made.

There are other advantages in building your own trailer out of a kit. As I have already mentioned, it is advisable to buy a trailer with a winch and suspensions arms rated above the minimum requirements for the weight of your boat. By building your own trailer it is possible to achieve this without having to pay extra to change these components on a standard-built trailer.

Most of the individual components supplied for self-assembly trailers bolt together and do not require welding. This allows anyone with basic DIY skills and a minimum of tools to build their own trailer. Apart from the advantage of an immediate cash saving, by putting it all together yourself you will have a greater appreciation of how everything works, which should make efficiently maintaining the trailer in a roadworthy condition a lot easier.

Buying a second-hand trailer

Buying a second-hand trailer is a perilous affair. Salt water is one of the most corrosive substances around and, even with plenty of maintenance, corrosion will very quickly attack all trailers. Components such as the winch, suspension units, jockey wheels and, especially, the hubs and wheel bearing require near-constant attention. After a few years they invariably require replacing but this depends on the amount of use.

Examine second-hand trailers thoroughly before you buy one. When the trailer is part of a package, you are really committed to buying it if you decide on the boat and engine. However, a thorough examination can quickly highlight defects on the trailer which can then be brought into the bartering process for the whole package. Be especially cautious when viewing a trailer that has been recently painted. A couple of strokes with a wire brush and a lick of Hammerite can quickly hide a multitude of defects, not least of which is severe corrosion.

I have yet to see a decent second-hand trailer offered for sale without a boat. First of all, you should fully satisfy yourself that any trailer offered minus a boat is not stolen. Think about it, why would anyone want to split up a boat and trailer package? Unless they plan on putting the boat into a marina, most trailers stay with the boat until they require replacing when they are often 'done up' with a coat of paint and offered to some unsuspecting buyer. Make sure this is not you!

2 Equipping your boat

Lighting

The lighting requirements for all vessels at sea are mandatory and precisely defined. The reasons why lighting requirements are so clearly defined are simple. When viewed from a distance they allow the trained navigator to determine the exact direction of travel, size and type of a vessel at night, allowing him to take any necessary avoiding action well in advance. Specific lighting requirements are laid down for all vessels at sea (Fig. 3).

I would recommend that all boat anglers buy a copy of an information-packed little booklet produced by the Royal Yachting Association, which contains a full set of 'rules of the road'. The book, ref. no. G2, is available from RYA House, Romsey Road, Eastleigh, Nr Southampton, Hampshire for a nominal charge. The legal lighting requirements for small fishing dinghies are as follows.

Rule 21 gives a very clear definition of each of the stipulated lights. Sidelights are defined as a green light on the starboard side and a red light on the port side, each showing an unbroken light over an arc of the horizon of 112.5 degrees, and so fixed to show the light from right ahead to 22.5 degrees abaft the beam on the respective side. In a vessel of less than 20 m (66 ft) in length the sidelights may be combined in one lantern carried on the fore and aft centreline of the vessel. An all-round light means a light showing an unbroken light over an arc of the horizon of 360 degrees.

Rule 22 stipulates the minimum range at which navigation lights for varying sized vessels shall be visible. Part C concerns vessels of less than 12 m (39 ft) in length, and states that an all-round light shall have a minimum range of visibility of 2 miles, and sidelights a minimum range of visibility of 1 mile.

Rule 23 then goes on to define which lights various different power-driven vessels shall display while underway. The term underway refers to any vessel that is not securely moored, anchored, aground or being towed, regardless of whether or not the engine is running, so this would include angling vessels fishing on the drift.

Part A states that a power-driven vessel underway shall exhibit:

i) a masthead light forward,

ii) a second masthead light abaft of and higher than the forward one; except that a vessel of less than 50 m (164 ft) in length shall not be obliged to exhibit such a light but may do so,

iii) sidelights,

iv) a sternlight.

Part C (i) of Rule 23 gives an exemption for power-driven vessels of less than 12 m (39 ft) in length, saying that they may in lieu of the light prescribed in Part A above of this rule exhibit an all-round white light and sidelights.

Part C (ii) of Rule 23 states: a power-driven vessel of less than 7 m (23 ft) in

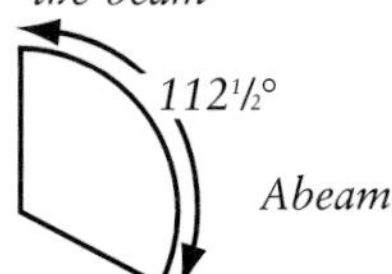

Lights for power-driven vessels underway (plan views)

Note *Also apply to sailing yachts or other sailing craft when under power*

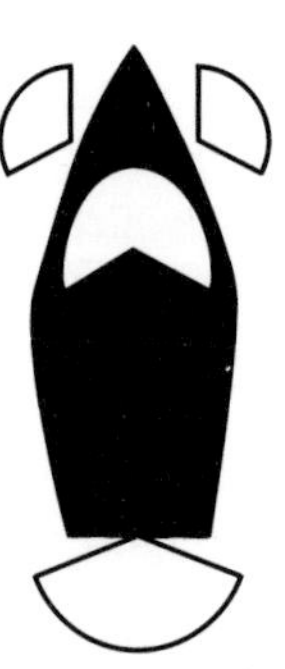

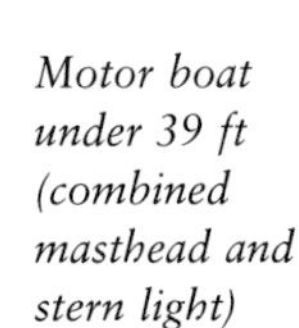

Fig. 3 Arcs and range of visibility of navigation lights.

length, and whose maximum speed does not exceed 7 knots may, in lieu of the lights prescribed in paragraph (a) of this rule, exhibit an all-round white light. Such a vessel *shall*, if practicable, also exhibit sidelights.

Rule 23 Part C (iii) gives a further exemption for vessels under 12 m (39 ft) in length, saying that the all-round white light need not be displayed on the centre-line of the vessel if this is not practicable, provided that the sidelights are combined in one lantern which shall be carried on the fore and aft centreline of the vessel, or located as nearly as practicable in the same fore and aft line as the masthead light or the all-round white light.

The lighting requirements for most fishing dinghies will be stipulated by the contents of Rule 23 (i), and thus require an all-round white light and sidelights.

Several companies produce suitable navigation lights. My own favourites, which are ideal for use aboard dinghies, are marketed by Aquamarine whose Series 25 lights are perfect for installation aboard most dinghies.

Electricity supply

Apart from the smallest inshore dinghies, most angling boats will require a simple 12-volt electrical circuit. An electrical supply will often be required to start an outboard engine and certainly required to run navigation lights and all other onboard electronics. The most simple set-up involves a single 12-volt battery connected to a fuse/switch box acting as a 'powerhead', from which items of electrical equipment can be fed. This sort of arrangement is perfectly adequate for many boats but it is not ideal.

A better system utilizes two batteries, one rigged purely to supply the engine, a second to run all other items of equipment. The obvious advantage of such a system is that there will always be a back-up battery onboard should any piece of equipment be accidentally left on, flattening one battery, and subsequently causing starting problems for the engine. Most modern outboards are designed to charge batteries while they are running.

Standard auto batteries are often used afloat but a leisure battery designed for use in caravans and boats, is a better, though far more expensive, choice. Auto batteries are full of highly corrosive acid which is all too easily tipped and spilt aboard a boat. Leisure batteries are filled with a gel and usually totally sealed. They make a far safer choice aboard high-speed boats, which have a tendency to shake about while underway. Unlike auto batteries, leisure batteries are designed to cope with long periods of inactivity without losing their charge.

If you do decide to opt for a cheaper auto battery, my advice would be to buy one recommended for cars of at least the size of a Cavalier or Mondeo. Fit it securely within the boat, being sure to cushion it adequately against vibration. Frequently check for terminal corrosion which should be removed with a wire brush; corrosion can be prevented by giving terminals a liberal coating of vaseline. Also, check the electrolyte level, topping up with distilled water as and when required. Periodically recharge the battery using a trickle charger.

The golden rules when installing an onboard electrical system are to keep the length of wiring and the numbers of connections to a minimum, and make sure that each and every component is individually fused with a suitably sized fuse as recommended by the manufacturer. You should also protect every connection from corrosion by keeping them well out of the way of salt-water spray and damp, backed up with a protective covering of vaseline.

Auxiliary means of propulsion

In addition to the main power unit, the dinghy angler will require some form of secondary means of propulsion. For those anglers with smaller dinghies who

Heading out to sea for a day's fishing. Note the spare engine mounted alongside the main engine, ready for immediate use.

Opposite **Crewsaver automatic lifejacket manufactured for Barbour. These jackets are ideal for fishing aboard small boats. They are very comfortable to wear and work in all day long and will automatically inflate within seconds should you fall into the water.**

concentrate on fishing inshore, a pair of good-quality wooden oars may well be suitable. However, rowing even a small boat for even a short distance in a choppy sea or against a running tide is an extremely arduous task and a back-up outboard engine will nearly always be preferred. If you do opt for oars, avoid plastic oars which are nearly always weak and of a poor quality. Also, make sure that your boat has a decent pair of galvanized rowlocks because plastic rowlocks have a tendency to flex and snap when put under pressure, especially in very hot or cold weather.

The size of the auxiliary outboard you buy should be governed by the distance that you usually fish offshore. For example, if you regularly fish in excess of five miles from your launch site, your return journey using a 2.2-h.p. plodder will take a long time and will be very uncomfortable in bad weather. A reliable 5-h.p. outboard will nearly always be a far more suitable choice aboard a dinghy and, if you fish at extreme range, I would give serious consideration to investing in a 10 h.p. or larger.

Far too many dinghy anglers simply store their spare engines out of the way until the day they need them. This is bad practice! Like all things mechanical, spare outboard engines should be regularly run and serviced, otherwise they will almost certainly deteriorate and fail when needed. The ideal place to store your auxiliary engine is on a bracket adjacent to the main engine so that it is ready for immediate use.

Lifejackets

At least one lifejacket should be provided for each person aboard the boat every time it goes to sea, regardless of how far out or for how long. There is a very big difference between a lifejacket and a cheaper buoyancy aid. A lifejacket has the necessary inherent buoyancy and is designed to turn an unconscious person so that they are kept face-up in the water. A buoyancy aid has only sufficient buoyancy to 'assist' a conscious adult to stay afloat: they are next to useless as items of safety equipment aboard offshore craft.

There are several excellent types of life-jackets on the market. My own favourites are produced by Crewsaver. When not activated, they resemble a waistcoat and can be worn in total comfort all day. The best jackets are designed to fully inflate instantly and automatically on contact with water – if, for example, you fall overboard. In addition, they can be

activated manually and topped up orally through a mouthpiece. Several other companies manufacture similar designs.

An increasing number of companies are producing flotation-type survival suits designed for anglers. By and large these are excellent and highly practical garments to wear while angling, as they also keep you warm and dry. However, not all suits on the market have the necessary buoyancy built in and need to be worn in conjunction with a lifejacket for adequate protection. Check before you buy!

Compass

No boat should ever put to sea without having a decent reliable compass aboard, regardless of other navigational equipment carried. The latest Global Positioning System (GPS) navigator is totally useless if the battery runs flat.

There are dozens of different types of compass on the market. The quality and accuracy of each is nearly always directly reflected by the price; in other words you only get what you pay for.

Expect to pay close to £50 for a reliable, magnetic compass. Look for a compass with at least a 3-in diameter display, marked in no less than 5-degree increments (Fig. 4). Anything smaller will make it next to impossible to steer to within 10 degrees of a set course over any sort of distance.

The better-quality compasses are designed to prevent the card spinning erratically at speed or in choppy seas. A backlight will be invaluable at night.

Be sure to fit the compass well out of the way of any possible magnetic and electrical interference and in such a position that it can be easily monitored in use.

Fig. 4 Typical fixed steering and hand-held bearing compass.

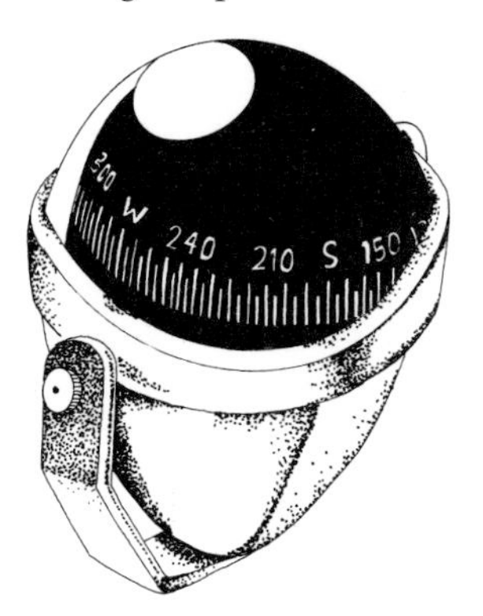

A fixed steering compass with a 3-in diameter and calibrated in 5-degree increments is the minimum suitable for use aboard a boat

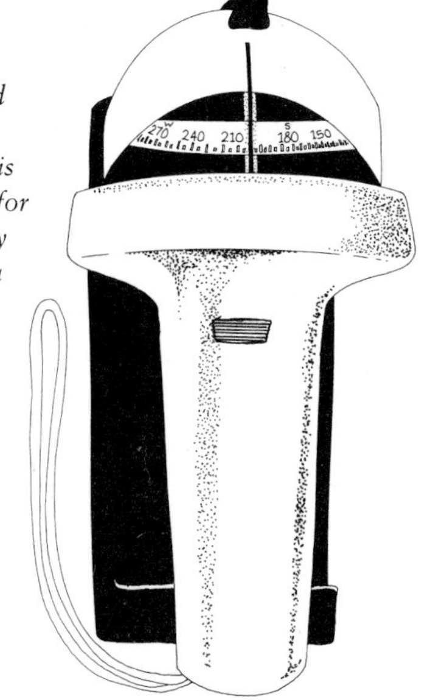

A quality hand-held bearing compass is essential for accurately plotting a boat's position

VHF radio

Not so long ago a marine VHF radio used to be considered a luxury aboard small private angling craft. Today prices have dropped considerably and I consider a VHF radio an essential item. The angler will be faced with the choice of either buying a hand-held portable VHF or a fixed set. The main difference between the two is that the power of a hand-held is restricted to 5 watts, occasionally 6 watts, but a fixed set will invariably have a full 25 watts of power.

Your choice should be governed by your style of fishing, as the amount of power in your radio will have a considerable effect on the efficiency and maximum transmission range of that set. A 5-watt hand-held radio will be perfectly adequate for transmitting over short distances under perfect conditions, but its effectiveness will be drastically reduced at times of adverse atmospherics or when transmitting in the vicinity of high cliffs.

If you fish inshore and off a busy part of the coast, with plenty of other boats in the area fitted with radios, a hand-held radio should be suitable. If, on the other hand, you fish off the west coast of Scotland or Ireland with a backdrop of high cliffs and few other boats in the area, or well offshore, then I strongly advise you to install a fixed 25-watt set for maximum transmission range.

In order to use a VHF you will need to pass an examination and obtain a licence. In addition, you will have to pay a fee to register the set with the Department of Trade. When installing a fixed VHF radio, be sure to fit a quality antenna, fixed as high as possible on the boat. The greater the height of the antenna, the greater the efficiency and effective transmission distance of that set.

Get in the habit of using your radio each and every time you go to sea. This serves three very important functions. Firstly, it confirms that the radio is both transmitting and receiving. Secondly, it is good practice to contact the coastguard before you set off, to tell him what sort of boat you are, what you intend to do, where you intend to go, how many persons are on board, and what time you anticipate returning. Lastly, only by regularly using the set will you become proficient and confident at operating it. An emergency is not the time to start blindly twiddling knobs and buttons in a panicked attempt at sending out a distress call.

Flares

All angling boats should be equipped with a full set of flares. For inshore work less than 3 miles from shore the coastguard recommends that you carry no less than two red hand-held flares and two hand-held orange smoke flares. For coastal work up to 7 miles offshore this is increased to 2 red hand-held flares, 2 hand-held orange smoke flares and 2 red parachute flares. For offshore work in excess of 7 miles from land this is increased to 4 red hand-held flares, 4 red parachute flares and 2 buoyant smoke flares. In addition, it is always worth carrying a few white anti-collision flares to attract attention to yourself if in danger of collision.

Flares do not have an infinite lifespan. Stamped on every flare will be an expiry date. Flares should not be kept or used beyond this date. The recommended way of disposing of out-of-date flares is to hand them in at either a coastguard or police station. Do not simply throw them in the bin or set them off on bonfire night. Used outside of a marine environment, distress flares can be extremely dangerous.

As all flares are pyrotechnics they should be stored carefully. The ideal container is an airtight plastic box, well padded out with old towels or foam to prevent the flares from rattling around inside. Read fully the operating instructions on each type of flare on a regular basis. Once again, an emergency situation is not the time to try and find out how to fire a flare safely.

A selection of hand-held flares.

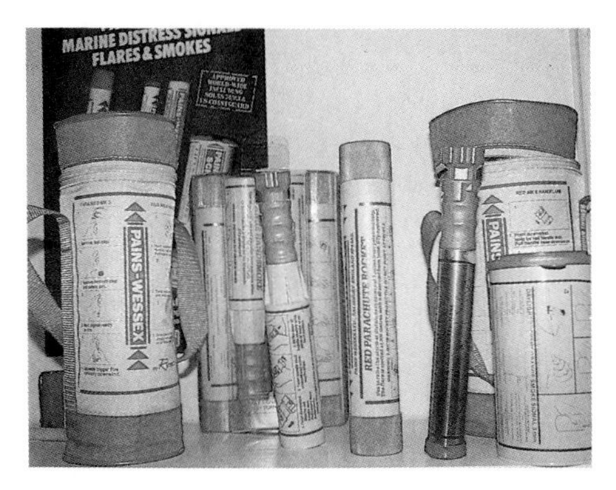

Depth sounder/fishfinder

It is hard to determine whether or not a fishfinder falls under the category of a luxury item or safety equipment. I suppose it lies somewhere in the middle. Nevertheless, it is rare these days to see an angling dinghy without a fishfinder of some description fitted aboard.

Several types of fishfinder are available, ranging from video sounders, and paper trace sounders, through to liquid crystal display (LCD) sounders. The latter are invariably the most suited for use aboard open angling dinghies, since in addition to providing a very concise and thorough display with all of the functions and features that any angler could ever need, most are waterproof.

You can buy a perfectly functional LCD fishfinder for under £150, but often by spending just £50 more you will get a far more versatile and useful unit. There are a multitude of features available on LCD sounders, and in all fairness, most models from most companies include the essential features.

One particularly useful feature found on products from the Eagle range is Greyline. Greyline helps to separate targets such as fish that are close to, or on, the bottom. Greyline also gives an indication of bottom hardness; for example, a seabed of hard rock would return a wide Greyline whereas one of soft mud would return a narrow Greyline. This can help the angler to deduce which types of fish are most likely to be in any given area.

Electronic navigators

Throughout the 1980s Decca was the system to have installed aboard fishing boats. When working correctly, the Decca system provided the high degree of accuracy necessary for boats to locate isolated marks well offshore and then return safely again in the event of poor visibility. Indeed, Decca is directly responsible for many great catches from offshore wrecks; but Decca has its problems. Transmission 'chains' suddenly break down, rendering the system all but useless, and Decca is notoriously temperamental at times of adverse atmospherics, notably around dusk and dawn when the fishing is often at its best.

At the start of the 90s, anglers were offered a spin-off benefit from the American 'Star Wars' program, in the form of an electronic navigation system known as Global Positioning System (GPS). The system utilizes transmissions from satellites out in space to give an

Eagle Supra Pro ID fishfinder in use with a portable power pack. An excellent piece of equipment with all of the functions and features that most anglers will ever need, ideal for use aboard fishing dinghies. Note the bilge pump fitted in the background.

extremely accurate position fix via a suitable receiver. The degree of accuracy can be controlled by the Americans, but it is guaranteed to provide a latitude and longitude fix of within 330 ft, usually much less. A system that intercepts the satellite signals then transmits an 'upgraded signal', known as Differential GPS (DGPS), is already with us, giving an almost unbelievable level of accuracy.

Unlike Decca, GPS is not affected by varying atmospherics and faulty transmitters and, despite the operators of Decca being granted a licence extending well into the next century, GPS is set to take over from Decca and become the onboard navigation system for the foreseeable future. Decca is set to follow the path of the dodo, and anyone planning to equip a boat need look no further than GPS, the price of which is falling by the month.

A top-of-the-range GPS set with combined fishfinder and plotter facilities, such as the Eagle Ultra Nav II, costs little more than £800, and hand-held GPS sets are available for as little as £300.

Most GPS sets have a memory facility in which hundreds of positions, or waypoints, as they are known, can be stored. Stored waypoints can be recalled simply by pressing a few buttons, and the precise course and distance to each is instantly displayed and constantly upgraded until that waypoint position is reached.

An additional feature on many GPS sets is a plotter. A plotter displays the boat's actual path relative to a fixed position. It is invaluable when drifting across either a reef or a wreck. By working in conjunction with a plotter it is possible accurately to pinpoint and 'home in' on productive parts of the drift, so that eventually you will be returning to the exact spot on each drift where the fish are feeding.

A man-overboard button is provided on most GPS sets. At the touch of the button the MOB position will be displayed, along with the course and distance back to that position. This is obviously a very useful safety feature to have aboard any boat.

First-aid kit

A basic first-aid kit is an obvious, though frequently overlooked, item of equipment to carry aboard a boat. Pre-packaged first-aid kits are readily available through car accessory shops and marine chandlers. For the same price or less you can often assemble your own first-aid kit, by buying individual items from a chemist and collecting them in an airtight box.

The sort of items that you should carry will include a roll of sticking plaster, which is far more practical and useful than individual plasters, a small pair of scissors, a tube of antiseptic cream, a

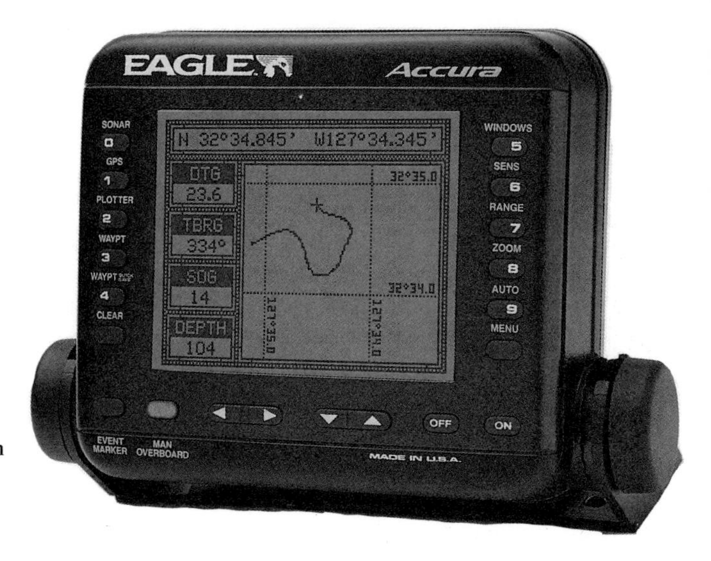

Eagle Accura GPS navigator. Shown with the plotting screen in use, an invaluable function when fishing on the drift.

selection of different sizes of dressings and bandages and a supply of aspirin or similar pain killers. Other items you think you might need can be easily added, especially if you require any special medication. It is also a good idea to obtain a book on first aid such as the one published by St Johns Ambulance Brigade, or, better still, to attend a first-aid course.

Spare parts and tool kit

A box of basic tools and a few spare parts are another sensible addition to the boat's safety inventory. Include both flat-head and cross-head screwdrivers, a spark plug spanner, a pair of pliers, an adjustable spanner, a sharp knife and a spare length of cord for starting the outboard engine if the pull cord fails. Plastic cable ties are invaluable for a whole range of tasks afloat, especially repairing damaged fuel lines. It might be worth including a small roll of electrical cable and a few connectors, and no boat should ever put to sea without having at least one large can of WD40 aboard. WD40 has saved the day for me many times over the years, from helping to start damp engines, freeing seized-up nuts and bolts and stopping those irritating little squeaks on fishing-reel handles that drive me mad!

Bilge pump/bailer

Depending on the design of the boat, either an electrical or a manual bilge pump, or both, should be installed. If your boat has sizeable compartments such as an engine hold or bilge below deck into which water can flood, then it is vital you install a reliable bilge pump. Electrical pumps are useful, but what happens in the event of a flat battery? Certainly install an automatically operated electrical pump to keep your boat afloat, but always back it up with a manual pump. At the very least always carry a hand bailer or bucket. A large sponge will be extremely useful for mopping up smaller quantities of water and generally helping to keep the boat clean.

Fog horn

All life jackets should be provided with a whistle for use in an emergency. An air canister-type fog horn is always worth having aboard for attracting attention in fog or an emergency. Keep it close at hand, ready for immediate use.

Spare clothes and food

Keeping a spare change of warm clothes, a few cans of drink and a few tins of food aboard is a wise precaution. You never know how long you might have to stay at sea if you break down, and hypothermia can set in very quickly if you are not prepared. Outdoor adventure shops stock a full range of survival food, including self-heating cans which are wonderful on a cold winter's day. Apart from providing a welcome hot meal they emit a tremendous amount of heat for a long time, which is great for warming your hands! Don't forget to carry a tin opener if you include cans of food.

Torch

A reliable torch with a spare bulb and batteries is another must, both as a convenience and for possible use to attract attention and to summon help.

EPIRB

An Emergency Position Indicating Radio Beacon (EPIRB) is another worthwhile consideration for anglers who fish well offshore. When activated, it transmits a distress signal that shipping, the coastguard and aircraft can pick up and locate. Several are now available at well under £100.

Spare anchor and warp

In addition to the main working anchor, always carry a fully rigged spare anchor ready for immediate use. Problems at sea have a tendency to compound themselves and escalate. Having sent out a distress signal, it is essential to remain in the same spot so that the various rescue services can locate you. If you have already lost an anchor, remaining in the same area is impossible without a spare.

Fire extinguisher

A good fire extinguisher is an essential, though often overlooked, item of safety equipment. Fire is potentially one of the worst situations that can arise at sea – after all, where can you run to on a 16-ft boat? Given the presence of fuel tanks, electrical wiring, batteries and the numerous other fire risks and ignition sources typically found aboard boats, a reliable fire extinguisher, capable of rapidly extinguishing a fire as soon as it is detected, is obviously essential.

The best type of extinguisher for use aboard most boats will be a stored pressure dry powder extinguisher. This is ideal for use on most types of fires, especially open petrol fires which could result following a spillage. Dry powder extinguishers, however, are extremely messy and for minor fires within a wheel house, fires involving electrical or electronic equipment, and fires in an enclosed engine hold, a carbon dioxide extinguisher might be better. Carbon dioxide will percolate behind panels and into inaccessible areas to extinguish a fire without causing any additional damage.

The ideal extinguisher to mount in an engine hold is an automatic CO_2 extinguisher, which will be immediately activated once a set temperature is exceeded – if the engine caught fire, for example – thus preventing the fire spreading.

Fire extinguishers should be replaced at the manufacturer's recommendations, and always kept close at hand. Read the operating instructions regularly, and follow them to the letter. Extinguishers are readily available through either chandlers or car accessory shops.

3 Safety and seamanship

Towing a boat

Towing a boat on the road forms a major part of modern dinghy fishing. When towing heavy loads along public roads it is easy to cause very serious accidents. For this reason I have decided to include a section devoted to safe towing.

Apart from the danger to life and limb (your own as well as those of other road users), and the risk of incurring a heavy penalty, neglecting to take adequate precautions before towing can easily result in severe damage to your boat. The hull of a boat is designed to withstand considerable amounts of stress and pressure, but only when the pressure is applied in a certain way. If too much pressure is put on certain localized parts of a GRP hull, the hull will easily break.

Boats should only be transported on trailers that are suitable for that particular design of hull. A well-designed trailer not only makes the task of launching and retrieving the boat as easy as possible, but it should also give plenty of support to the hull during road transit. I have already covered the points to consider when matching a boat with a suitable trailer (see pp. 10–12). However, the trailer alone will not support the boat securely enough for safe road transit. There are several other precautions that boat owners should take whenever the boat is towed, including a few legal requirements.

It is essential that the boat is securely strapped on to the trailer. A good, wide webbing strap will prevent the boat from getting shaken about on the trailer, possibly vibrating the keel off the rollers. Serious damage to the hull can all too easily be caused at its point of contact with the side supports, due to bouncing on uneven road surfaces. A strap will also hold the boat secure in high winds, especially when turning sharp corners or roundabouts, or when large lorries are overtaking you on a motorway.

There are plenty of different types of trailer straps available on the market. These straps have been designed specifically for securing boats on to trailers. The better ones are of webbing and at least 1 in wide. The width of the strap is important. A wide strap will grip far better and with far less tendency to cut into the boat than a narrow one. In addition, a wide strap will offer more resistance to vibration-induced movement than a narrow strap, or a length of rope.

On most boats, the best place to position the strap is above the trailer's axle, which is usually situated below the broadest part of the trailer. The strap is held in place on either side of the trailer with metal hooks, attached to suitable anchor points on the trailer. Tensioning the strap is easy. All slack is first pulled through by hand. Then the buckle or ratchet is snapped over with a lever action applying the final tension. With straps that are tensioned with a ratchet mechanism, take great care to prevent over-tightening, which could damage the hull as a result of excessive pressure crushing it.

It is also good practice to protect the hull from abrasion, caused by the strap at all points where it is in contact with the fibreglass. In time, an unprotected strap can wear away the gel coat. Use old strips of foam-backed carpet, rubber, or towels, especially beneath the tensioning buckle. When towing for any great distance it is a good idea to pull over and check the strap at regular intervals, adjusting any slack.

It is very important to prevent the bow of the boat from bouncing while on the road. This is easily achieved using the winch strap or rope. After winching the boat completely back on to the trailer, unclip the strap and pass it under the trailer grab handles, then re-clip it back on to the boat's winching eye. A couple of turns of the winch handle will securely clamp the bow firmly down on to the trailer against the rubber buffer, which is fitted to the winch post. Again be careful not to over-tighten, and protect the strap or rope from abrasion as before.

I always chain my trailer to the car ball hitch. When left unattended, this acts as a simple, yet effective deterrent against theft, and ensures that, should the coupling and ball hitch separate while on the road, the trailer will remain attached to the towing vehicle (Fig. 5).

The law demands an approved and fully operational lighting set is attached at the rear end of the trailer. Lighting boards are readily available through car accessory shops, where they cost considerably less than an identical product at the chandlers. The trouble is they never seem to last for long before the lights start playing up.

The lifespan of a lighting board can be increased by keeping it away from salt water. Remove it from the boat and stow it in a garage or shed when not in use, and frequently check and clean all connections with fine wet and dry sandpaper. Finish by applying a protective spray of WD40. Check your lights prior to every trip, as towing a boat with defective lights will result in a fine and points on your driving licence.

The law also requires that all 'dangerous projections' are suitably covered and clearly visible. This includes both outboard engine and stern drives. The easy solution here is to buy a purpose-made propeller bag, costing around £10. This will ensure that you tow within the law, as well as protect the propeller and lower

Fig. 5 Method of chaining a trailer to ball hitch for additional security.

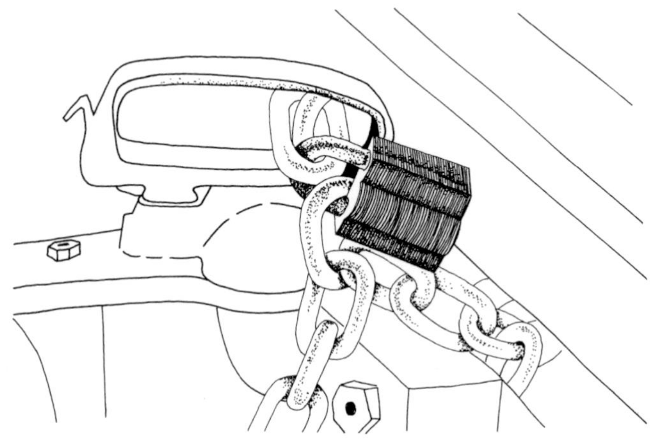

A quality chain and padlock used to secure a boat trailer to the tow hitch is not only a wise safety precaution – it can prevent the theft of the trailer when you are fishing at sea

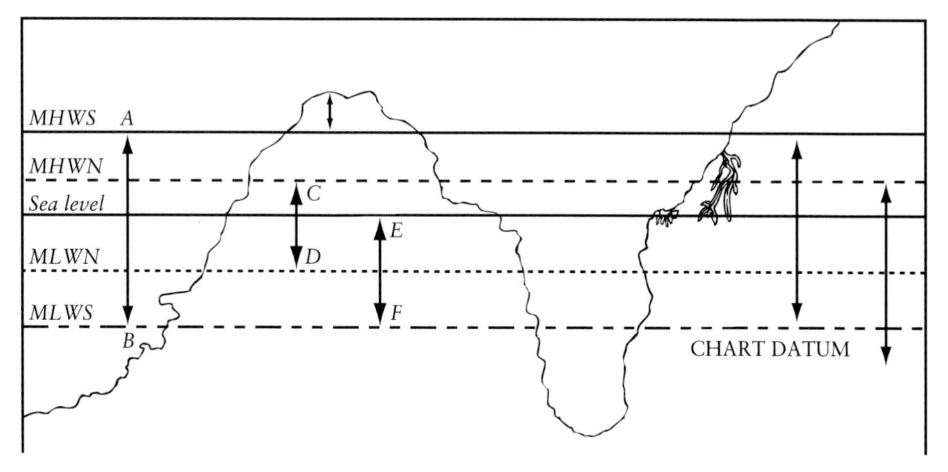

A B = spring-tide range
C D = neap-tide range
E F = actual height of tide

MHWS = mean high water spring height
MLWS = mean low water spring height
MHWN = mean high water neap height
MLWN = mean low water neap height

Fig. 6 Diagram showing cross-section of tidal range during different heights of tide.

leg from chips caused as a result of stones thrown up off the road. These bags are readily available through all chandlers.

Mudguards are another legal requirement. An increasing number of trailers are fitted with plastic mudguards which have a very short lifespan, usually cracking the first time someone uses them to climb aboard the boat. Again, it is in your own interests to ensure that the mudguards are in a good condition; if they are not, stones will quickly damage your boat's gel coat.

Always check that the trailer jockey wheel is fully housed before road transit. Jockey wheels can easily work loose on long road journeys, resulting in damage when you drive over a hump in the road such as speed ramps.

It is very important that the wheel bearings are regularly serviced, the trailer tyres are in good condition and the overall standard of the trailer is sound and intact. Failure to observe all of these recommendations and requirements will be costly, with a high risk of unnecessary repair costs, big fines, points on your driving licence and lost fishing time.

Tides (Fig. 6)

It is very important for the dinghy angler to appreciate the effect different heights of tides can have on sea conditions in the area in which they fish. For example, one week's fishing might coincide with a set of small neap-tides. With a south-westerly wind of, say, 15 knots blowing against the tide, conditions offshore might be both comfortable and safe. However, the following week's spring-tides might well be a totally different proposition, with the same strength of wind throwing up a rough sea in a developing wind-over-tide situation.

During spring-tides a far greater volume of water moves within the same time period as during the smaller neaps. Obviously this equates to a much stronger run of tide, which, apart from affecting the fishing, can very quickly create a disturbed and violent sea, especially around exposed headlands where the run of tide is usually strongest.

When the wind is blowing in the same direction as a spring-tide the sea can often be glassy calm. However, when the tide turns against the direction of the wind even a light breeze can create a rough sea, and when you are in a 16-ft boat, it can be extremely unnerving and uncomfortable. Anticipating how a change of tide can alter the effect of the prevailing wind is the key to safe dinghy fishing.

The various heights and times of tides is governed by the moon and its lunar orbit in relation to earth. Spring-tides, the biggest tides of the month, coincide with either a new moon or a full moon, when the gravitational pull on the earth is at its strongest.

Friction against the coastline retards the tidal action so that a place which is connected with the main ocean by long channels, such as the eastern end of the Bristol Channel, will not experience the highest tides on the actual day of the new or full moon, but perhaps two days later. This delay is called the 'age of the tide'.

Neap-tides fall midway between each sequence of springs. One week after a new moon we will see approximately a quarter of the moon in the sky; this is the first quarter. Two weeks later we will see the opposite quarter of the moon; the tides are now said to be in the last quarter.

Weather forecasts

No angler should ever put to sea without having received the very latest weather forecast. Weather patterns in the United Kingdom are a best unpredictable, and a day that dawns fine and sunny can all too often end with a full-blown gale.

There are many sources from which accurate weather forecasts can be obtained. Weather bulletins at the end of television news programmes are popular with anglers, in particular the weekend outlook given after the Wednesday BBC1 lunchtime news, and the week's forecast for farmers and growers on BBC1 on a Sunday lunchtime. National forecasts should be checked by watching local weather reports broadcast after local news programmes. Shipping forecasts for the various sea areas are broadcast on BBC radio programmes throughout the day and full details of their times are in *Radio Times*.

Coastguard stations broadcast the local inshore weather forecast at various intervals throughout the day on VHF; it includes the present sea conditions. The coastguards are more than willing to give the latest weather information if you phone them prior to sailing, or call them on a VHF radio.

Many popular angling magazines run a telephone weather/fishing information service, notably *Sea Angler* magazine's *Coastcall* (on 0891 600 262), which provides up-to-date information on coastal weather and sea conditions around the country. Daily forecasts are available from 0600 hours every Friday, Saturday and Sunday, and all English Bank Holidays. Every Monday a comprehensive weekly forecast for the entire United Kingdom is available. It should be remembered that this service should not be regarded as a replacement for the local coastguard report or other sources of local weather information.

Engine failure at sea

Regardless of how well you maintain and look after your boat's engine, one day it will probably let you down. With proper maintenance the sort of problems you will encounter will, it is hoped, be minor ones, easily rectified on the spot. Each year many boat anglers run into problems which could, and should, have been avoided and could have been solved on the spot if they had only stopped for a minute to think the problem through.

Most engine problems are minor ones and can easily be cured at sea. The first thing you should do in the event of main engine failure at sea is to let someone know you have got a problem. This does not mean setting off flares or sending Mayday messages, unless, of course, you are in any sort of danger. It is to be hoped that you have a VHF radio aboard. Use it to contact friends or other fishing boats in the area and tell them your engine has failed. Always give your present position. If you are out on your own, use the VHF to notify the coastguard, who will be able to monitor your situation closely, ready to instigate a recovery operation if required.

If the boat is drifting, drop the anchor and note your position with land bearings, or write the position down if you have a navigator aboard. At least if the situation deteriorates and you are unable to start your engine, or if fog develops, you will have a record of your position.

Ideally you will have a spare engine or at the very least oars. If not, why not? If the spare is carried on the transom, start it up. If your spare is stowed out of the way then get it out and ready for immediate use. Now is the time to start examining your main engine.

Most instances of outboard engines failing to start can be traced back to faults on either the engine's fuel or electrical systems and, depending on the symptoms, these should be the first areas to look at when trying to establish the cause of the problem.

It is surprising how many people run out of petrol, then spend a lot of time looking for faults before they realize what has happened. If you are using a lot of fuel try to change tanks before they run dry. Most tanks have an amount of sediment in the bottom, which can get drawn into the system, along with air, when the fuel level is allowed to get too low, causing blockages.

If your engine initially started easily and then cut out within a short distance of the harbour or launch site, check the fuel delivery system. A common cause for this sort of problem is forgetting to open the vent on the fuel tank. As your engine uses fuel, the level in the tank, which should be air tight, drops. If this displaced volume is not replaced with air a vacuum will eventually develop, stopping the fuel passing through to the engine. Opening the tank vent prevents this from happening.

Air locks within the fuel system are another common fault. Generally these are easily cleared by pumping the priming bulb in the fuel line. When you do get the engine running after such a fault has occurred, leave it ticking over at moderate revs for a minute or so to ensure that the entire fuel system is fully primed. Immediate application of full throttle will nearly always lead to its cutting out again.

If your fuel delivery system has developed a leak it will nearly always become instantly apparent from the strong smell of petrol. Most fuel leaks occur at joints. Repairing them is usually a simple case of disconnecting and trimming back the fuel line and then reconnecting it. Plastic cable ties are excellent for joining fuel lines and should be included in every spares kit (see p. 21).

Flat batteries are a frequent cause of trouble afloat. The ideal boat's electrical system should be fitted with a pair of batteries, which can be isolated in turn with a switch. As an alternative, fit one battery to run the engine components and a second for lighting and electronics.

It is surprising how many boat owners do not realize that, even when the battery is flat, the engine can usually be started by hand. Ensure the ignition is turned on and the choke out if the engine is cold, then pull the starting cord with smooth firm pulls. If the engine is not fitted with a recoil start, remove the engine cover and wrap a cord around the fly wheel as detailed in the engine manual. It is generally only the larger engines that have no facility for manual starting. This is a useful exercise to practise one day, perhaps when the fishing is poor, as it is always better fully to familiarize yourself with emergency procedures before you have to attempt things under pressure.

An engine failing to start may be nothing more than a blown fuse. Check all inline fuses straight away and replace any that have blown with a new fuse of similar ampage rating: never use a higher rating. If this fuse blows again there is a fault on the system. This will have to be sorted out before you can use the engine.

Overchoking a warm engine will also prevent it starting. At the start of the day you may well need to use the full amount of choke to get an engine running, but if you have only been anchored for a couple of hours' fishing you will rarely need the same amount of choke to restart, unless, of course, the weather is particularly cold.

If you do flood the engine, turn it over a few times with the choke in, so as to try and clear the system and get it to fire. When it does show signs of life, apply a small amount of throttle and choke. When you do manage to get it running, leave it running for a couple of minutes to warm through and burn off any excess fuel before you apply the throttle.

If the engine still refuses to show signs of life, remove the spark plugs and give them a good cleaning with a soft wire brush. You should have a spare set of plugs afloat with you; it may be worth fitting these. At least you can then be sure it is not a simple plug fault.

Other ignition components which are likely to break down at sea are CDI ignition units, coils, etc. Unfortunately there is not a lot the average man can do about these out on the water so it will usually be a case of finding an alternative way back.

Problems with damp are not common once an engine has been running. Some engines are more prone to damp problems than others and a quick squirt with WD40 or a marine alternative may help.

Different makes and models of outboard engine all have their little peculiarities which prevent them from starting from time to time. Familiarity with your engine is the key to sorting these problems out. A comprehensive maintenance manual, complete with trouble-shooting chart, and a tool kit and spares are essential. With a little time and logical thinking most of the problems listed above can be very easily rectified. Just imagine the embarrassment of having to instigate a full air and sea rescue just because you had run out of petrol, left the fuel tank cap vent closed or left the choke out!

Anchoring

There is more to anchoring a dinghy safely and efficiently than simply throwing a rope with anchor attached over the side, then waiting for the tide or wind to position the boat. There is a right and wrong way to anchor a boat, get it wrong and you can end up with all sorts of problems, the rapid sinking of your boat topping the list.

You should first ensure that you buy an anchor suitable for the area you intend fishing and for the size of boat. There is no such thing as an all-round anchor, but

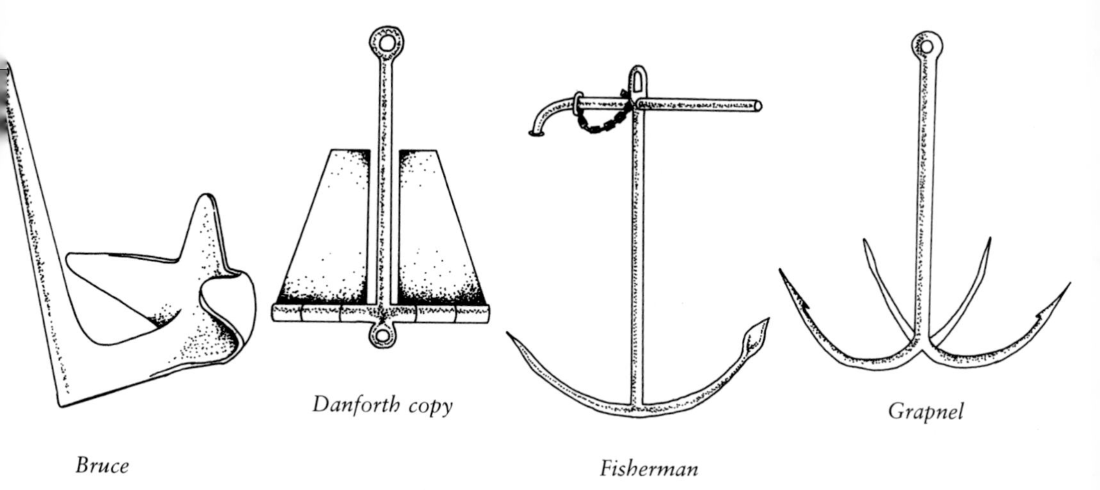

Fig. 7 Selection of four different types of anchor.

one or two designs come close within the context of dinghy fishing. A suitable anchor is one which will hold the boat where you intend it to be held, not just one which folds away neatly for easy stowage.

Several designs are recommended for use on dinghies (Fig. 7). A simple grapnel or a Danforth are both anchors which will hold firm over a variety of different types of seabed. The Bruce anchor is also very efficient but expensive. The traditional fisherman pattern is widely seen aboard dinghies, yet in the lighter weights it is not an anchor which is particularly efficient. Over a rocky or firm bottom the fisherman will hold well, but over cleaner ground of either mud or sand it has a tendency to slide before holding fast. This can result in the boat moving away from the intended mark and the anchor eventually snagging.

If you decide on a grapnel, forget those neat little folding anchors, which are widely available and widely used by the water skiing and yachting fraternity. The holding qualities of these anchors are inadequate over all but the roughest seabeds and I would suggest that they are usually bought for their neatness rather than their efficiency. If you fish over wrecks or a particularly snaggy seabed, then a home-made grapnel is both a cheap and practical choice of anchor.

An anchor of about 16 lb in weight is about right for a 16-ft dinghy, with approximately 1 lb of weight per foot of boat being a general recommendation. Today many manufacturers produce lightweight aluminium anchors which are very effective and easy to handle. At the end of the day it is often the design rather than the weight of the anchor that counts.

An anchor should be considered not just as a piece of equipment to hold a boat on a fishing mark, but more as a potential lifesaver. If the engine fails as you are passing a rocky headland with wind and tide setting landwards, only a good anchor is going to stop the boat from drifting on to the rocks. Or with wind and tide pushing you offshore into deeper water, this is not the time to discover that in 120 ft of water over a bottom of hard flat sand your anchor won't hold, or that you have insufficient anchor rope aboard.

There are various methods of rigging anchors so that they can trip and be pulled free if they snag. The most common is when the bottom of the anchor instead of the top is secured to the end of the anchor chain. The chain is laid along the shaft of the anchor and secured at the normal fastening point with weak cord, such as fishing line or nylon cable ties. If the anchor becomes snagged, pulling carefully from different angles, with the boat's engine, causes this weak link to break, allowing the anchor to be pulled out in the opposite direction.

This can be a useful method which prevents losses if you regularly anchor over snaggy ground or wrecks. Great care should always be exercised when applying a load to a small boat as you attempt to break out the anchor. Also, it is advisable always to carry at least one anchor rigged in the normal way for use in emergencies, when it is imperative to stop the boat drifting into danger.

Polypropylene is the material by far the most widely used by fishermen for their anchor ropes, but has its limitations, the major one being that it floats. Care needs to be observed at times of slack water to prevent yards and yards of rope floating on the surface. Nylon ropes sink, but are a lot more expensive than polypropylene.

Floating ropes are an obvious risk to other boats in the vicinity. However, the biggest hazard with a floating rope is

Fig. 8 Correct method of attaching anchor rope to chain using a thimble and eye splice.

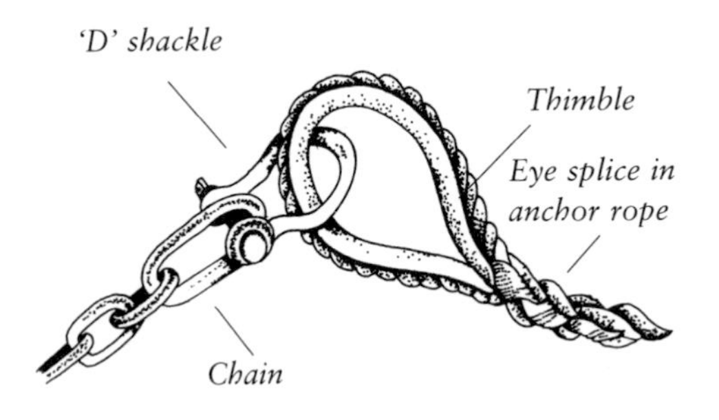

the risk of its fouling the engine's shaft or propeller, especially if it is not noticed. As the tide increases in strength the boat can then end up anchored stern into the flow of water. This is a very dangerous situation and not quickly rectified in a strong tide without resorting to the knife, which should be used without delay to free the rope.

A rope with about a ½ in diameter will suit most dinghy situations. Any thinner than this and it becomes uncomfortable on the hands and will cut into them as you retrieve the anchor. Any thicker and the tide will exert a much greater pressure on the rope, thus reducing the effectiveness of the anchor.

A length of chain should be used to join an anchor to the main rope; 12 ft of galvanized chain is about right for a typical 16-ft dinghy. The chain serves the purpose of assisting the anchor to take hold by helping maintain a horizontal pull along the seabed because of its extra weight. Chain also avoids wear on the lower part of the main rope resulting from contact with rocks.

The chain should be attached to the anchor using a decent galvanized shackle and to the rope by means of an eye-splice tied around a galvanized thimble and using a second shackle (Fig. 8). Never tie or splice a rope directly to the chain. In no time at all constant tension and abrasion, where the rope and chain join, will cause wear, a sure way of losing both anchor and chain.

The rule of thumb for deciding on the length of anchor rope is to carry a length equal to three times the maximum depth of water in your area; then, when you anchor, you can use three times the depth of water in rope. For example, if you are fishing in 30 ft of water, release approximately 90 ft of rope. In many situations

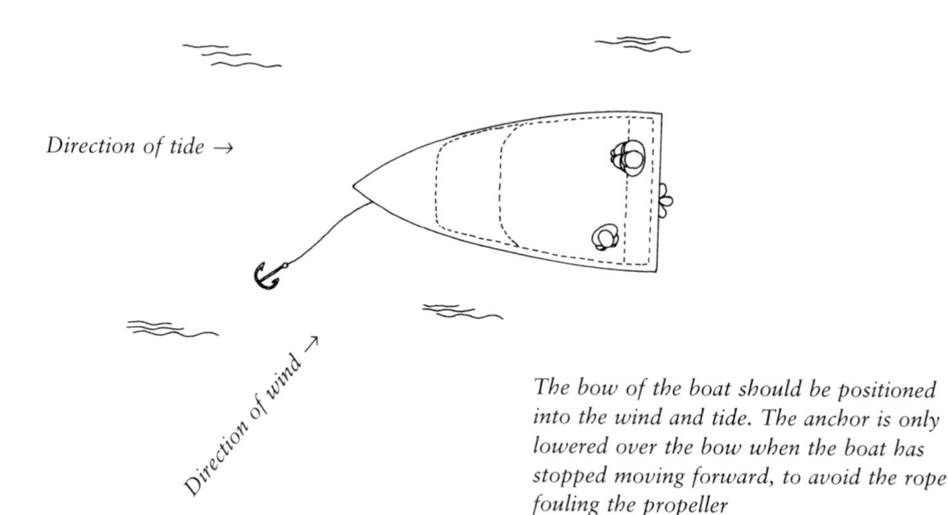

Fig. 9 Correct method of anchoring, bow into wind and tide.

using three times the depth of water in rope will be adequate, but be prepared to pay out additional rope in very strong tides, especially in deep water. I would recommend buying a rope long enough to give you at least four times the maximum depth of water in your area; you will rarely, if ever, need to use it all, but it will always be available.

A large buoy should be attached to the other end of the anchor rope; this is an essential piece of equipment. It allows you to slip the anchor in a hurry, then return to the buoy and retrieve it. This might be a necessary manoeuvre if, for example, a passing ship has not seen you sitting at anchor, or if a favourite fishing hat gets blown over the side!

The actual anchoring process is straightforward. The boat is positioned with its bow pointing in the direction it is anticipated it will end up lying at anchor. This is determined by the strength and direction of the tide and the wind. When the boat has stopped moving forward the anchor is carefully lowered over the side. Never throw it as the chain or warp can very easily tangle around the anchor flukes. Allow the anchor to fall swiftly to the bottom, letting the tide and wind push the boat away from the anchor. At times of slack tide it can be helpful to run the boat slowly astern with the engine (Fig. 9).

When the boat is clearly running away from the anchor, gradually increase the tension on the rope. This will assist the anchor to bite into the seabed. When the rope is lying at an angle of approximately 45 degrees from the bow to the bottom, hold the rope firmly. If the anchor has not gripped you will feel it dragging across the bottom. Let out some more rope and hold it firmly again. Eventually, provided that you have followed all of the guidelines above, the anchor will grip.

There are several methods of retrieving anchors. Always start the engine before you haul the anchor and be careful to ensure the boat does not pass over the top of the rope, possibly resulting in its fouling around the engine or keel.

An increasingly popular method of retrieving an anchor, which eliminates much of the graft of hand hauling, is rigging it so that it can be broken out and raised to the surface using the engine and a large floating buoy. The method is known as the Alderney Ring method (Fig. 10).

A buoy of about 20 in diameter is attached to a couple of feet of rope. A metal ring about 6 in diameter, large enough to pass easily over any shackles or chain, is attached to the other end and threaded on to the main anchor warp.

At the start of the day, release the anchor, ensuring you keep hold of the metal ring thus allowing the rope to pass easily through it. When sufficient warp is out the warp is made fast and the buoy attached to the ring by a spring clip and dropped into the water.

To retrieve the anchor, the boat is run

Fig. 10 Retrieving a Bruce-type anchor using the Alderney Ring method.

ahead at an angle to the anchor warp, exercising extreme care not to foul the engine with the rope. The rope passes through the metal ring, and the floating buoy is forced down the rope. A combination of engine power and the buoyancy of the buoy raises the anchor to the surface, where it will lie inside the ring. In the mean time you should have retrieved the slack anchor rope into the boat. When the anchor is on the surface it can easily be brought alongside the boat and lifted aboard.

I would not recommend this method to anyone who is not totally confident in handling their boat. In choppy seas, in poor light, and if attempted by a novice aboard an unsuitable or weak boat, this can be a dangerous method. I know of several instances where, as a direct result of bad seamanship, boats have sunk as a result of the rope fouling the engine. If you must try it, get plenty of practice in sheltered water on a flat calm day with no tide before you attempt it at any other time. The safest way to retrieve an anchor aboard a small boat is by hand, hauling it over a bow roller, thus keeping the boat positioned bow into the wind and tide.

Man overboard procedures

There will always be a risk of losing someone overboard when fishing from a small boat, and it will be the initial actions of the person at the wheel which will determine whether or not the incident is quickly resolved or becomes more serious.

It needs to be said that it is good practice always to wear a lifejacket when afloat. In reality few of us do, but I for one will always don a lifejacket whenever fishing at night or in anything other than calm seas. In the event of falling overboard and sustaining an injury, a lifejacket will maintain an unconscious adult with his or her face clear of the water.

In the event of someone falling overboard, the helmsperson's first reaction should be instantly to turn the wheel in the direction that the person has fallen and to cut the revs, thus turning the propeller away from the casualty. If the person falls over on the starboard side, then the wheel is locked over to starboard. If he or she falls over on the port side then the wheel is locked over to port.

If there is another person aboard the boat he or she should keep a constant watch on the casualty's position, pointing

By far the safest way of hauling an anchor aboard a small boat; by hand straight over a bow roller, thus keeping the boat heading into the tide and the rope well clear of the propeller.

in their direction to keep the casualty in view. If the boat is fitted with a navigator, then the MOB button should be pressed at the first possible instant. If a lifebuoy is carried then this should be thrown towards the casualty as soon as possible. The coastguard should also be informed immediately; after all, what would happen if you fell into the water trying to lift the other person out?

The person at the helm should carefully manoeuvre the boat around the casualty to approach from downtide or downwind, whichever is the stronger. If an attempt is made to approach from either uptide or upwind then there is a serious risk of the boat running over the person in the water.

The final approach to the casualty should be made with extreme caution, and made so that the boat is more or less stopped as he or she comes into reach. Manoeuvre the boat so that the casualty comes alongside approximately midships on either the port or starboard side, whichever offers the best visibility for the helmsperson. If the casualty is conscious and able to assist themselves then carefully offer them a boat hook or get them to swim the last few feet towards the boat. The engine should now be in neutral, to eliminate any chance of causing an injury with the propeller.

Assist the casualty in getting aboard. The risk of hypothermia should never be ignored after even short periods of immersion, especially in winter. If you carry some old towels and dry clothes (always a good idea as most of us get wet now and again during launching and retrieving) these should be provided. If not, then an immediate return to land should be considered.

Night fishing

Before too long, most dinghy anglers will consider fishing at night. Night fishing for certain species in certain areas can be very rewarding, especially in shallow, clear water. In other areas with deep, coloured water, fishing during the hours of darkness may be no more productive than fishing during daylight. Also, it is often the dawn and dusk periods that tend to be the most productive, not the midnight hours. That said, you will probably be tempted to try a night trip, especially during the winter with shorter days.

My advice to the novice dinghy angler would be to forget all thoughts of fishing at night until you have at least a full

year's experience of daylight fishing. Never fish at night in any area that you have not fished extensively during daylight, and certainly not in an area where there are an adundance of hazards such as shallow reefs, rock pinnacles, tide rips, shipping lanes, moorings or pot markers.

When you do decide to give night fishing a try, pick your day carefully. Choose a flat, calm day, with excellent visibility. Even a short chop that wouldn't worry you during the day can cause concern at night. Fishing at night and during fog or mist can be a recipe for disaster.

Select a few safe inshore marks to fish, preferably within a short steaming distance from your launch site. It is always a good idea to start off fishing during daylight and then settle on the chosen mark before darkness falls, rather than set off in pitch black. Always wear a lifejacket when fishing at night.

A reliable lighting source is both a convenience and a comfort, plus an essential safety, and legal, requirement. Never use either paraffin or petrol lights afloat, for obvious reasons. Ideally you will have an efficient lighting arrangement run from the boat's own power supply, backed up with a separate portable battery-operated supply, complete with spare batteries. The ideal lighting arrangement will be powered by a totally separate battery to the battery that starts the boat's engine. Strip lights are more efficient than spot lamps, and use far less power.

Temperatures at night fall rapidly, so take plenty of spare clothing, hot drinks and food. Always make sure that someone, preferably the coastguard, knows where you are fishing. Viewed from the shore, a person continually moving backwards and forwards in front of a light can look like a boat in distress signalling for help. The coastguard frequently has to deal with false alarms caused in this way.

Night fishing can be very productive, but the best results are often around dusk and dawn.

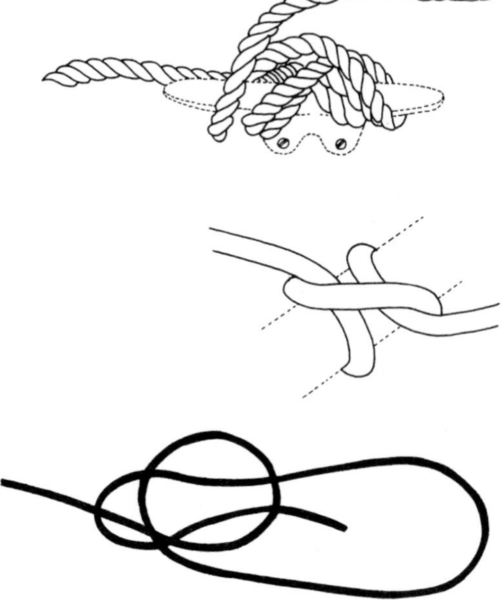

Method of tying anchor off into a cleat using 3 or 4 figure-of-eight turns

Clove hitch: a good all-round knot for tying off on to a rail etc.

Bowline: used to tie a strong loop in a line

Fig. 11 Selection of useful boating knots.

Always keep a very good look-out for other boats in your area when fishing at night, or in restricted visibility, no matter how well lit you think you are. You could be obscured from a distance by your lights blending into a background of lights on the shore.

Lastly, always proceed at vastly reduced speeds at night compared with the speed you would adopt during daylight. Even a small lump of timber can hole a GRP hull if hit at speed, and a pot marker or mooring wrapped around the propeller could spell disaster at night.

I have already mentioned the danger of allowing an anchor rope to foul the engine shaft or propeller. Even in a light tide and slight sea, this is one of the worst problems that can develop aboard. In a very short time the stern of the boat can be dragged under water, resulting in the rapid swamping of the boat's cockpit. Always take every possible precaution to prevent this happening. If it does, never hesitate in cutting the rope if it cannot be immediately cleared by lifting the engine.

For the reasons given above, a boat should always be anchored from the bow, never the stern or midships. Tie the warp off using a series of figure-of-eight knots around a cleat or similar deck fitting; then finish off with a half hitch over the top of the cleat. The warp should preferably run over a roller. Four or five turns will both hold the boat fast and ensure easy release. Any other knot will invariably jam with the constant pressure and jarring, and prove difficult to untie, possibly damaging the warp (Fig. 11).

The anchor should always be stowed away neatly. A fish box or cut-down plastic drum is ideal, with the rope neatly coiled inside it. The vast majority of rope available is right-hand lay, which should be coiled clockwise inside the box, where it will form neat coils. Try and coil it in an anticlockwise direction and the result will be a box of twisted and kinked rope which will not pay out neatly the next time you come to use it.

4 Navigation

Small boat navigation today relies more on the accurate interpretation and use of the information extracted from electronic instruments, than on the use of compass bearings, parallel rulers and dividers for plotting and calculating positions and courses. Yet, a sound knowledge of the basics of navigation is still essential. Without a basic understanding of the principles of navigation it is impossible to feed the various types of navigators with the information required for them to work accurately, or to fully utilize the information provided by them.

The newcomer to boat ownership should learn how to use all of the various items of navigation equipment fitted aboard his boat, starting with a sound working knowledge of an Admiralty sea chart. He must learn how to extract the exact positions from that chart in latitude and longitude, and how to plot positions on to it. He or she will need to learn how to plot courses between different points and how to read and lay off bearings from buoys or other land marks.

A chart will both assist the angler's safe passage and help to locate productive fishing grounds. Indeed, a good chart provides such a wealth of information to the angler that even when fishing an area for the first time, a quick look at the seabed topography will quickly reveal many likely fish-holding areas.

The earth's surface is divided up by imaginary lines which are called lines of latitude and longitude. The lines which run north to south are called lines of longitude, and are measured as being either east or west of the Greenwich Meridian. This is 0 degree longitude and is the line running south from the North Pole through Greenwich in London, down to the South Pole. Longitude is measured as being the angle between Greenwich, the centre of the earth and any point on the earth's surface.

Lines which run around the earth surface parallel to the Equator are termed lines of latitude. These are measured through an arc of 90 degrees, from the Equator to the centre of the earth and then to the given point on the earth's surface. The Equator has a latitude of 0 degrees, with the respective poles being 90 degrees north and south (Fig. 12).

Positions are plotted using these two co-ordinates. Around the UK the latitude will always be north, but if you are working off the south-east coast, always ensure that you check whether or not your position or planned course takes you east or west of the Greenwich meridian.

There are 90 degrees of latitude in both the northern and the southern hemisphere, and 180 degrees of longitude in both the eastern and the western hemisphere. The degrees are further subdivided into 60 smaller units known as minutes. For standard inshore chart work

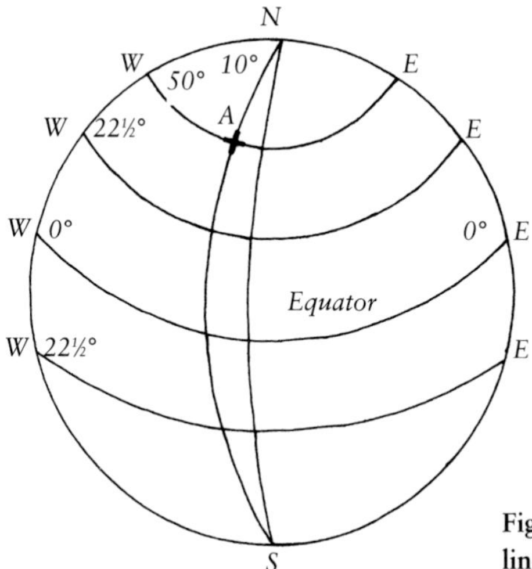

W→E lines of latitude
N→S lines of longitude
Position A = Lat 50°N, Long 10°W

Fig. 12 Diagram of the earth showing lines of latitude and longitude.

the minutes are further split into tenths, known as cables.

Latitude is read off either the right- or left-hand scale on the chart, longitude off either the top or bottom scale. Distance can also be calculated from the latitude scale, one minute of latitude being the equivalent of one nautical mile in that latitude. Latitude and distance should always be measured using the latitude scale nearest to the area where you are operating. The length of one minute of latitude decreases as you progress further north or south. This is the reason why the latitude scale, adjacent to the position where you are working, should always be used for measuring distances. The standard nautical mile is taken as being 6076 ft, which is the equivalent of one minute of latitude in the English Channel.

Transferring positions on and off the chart is achieved by using either a pair of parallel rulers, or a pair of pointed dividers, which many find the easier and most accurate method aboard a small boat. The dividers are opened to the distance between the mark and the nearest permanent line of latitude or longitude drawn on the chart, and, being very careful not to move the setting, they are transferred across to the chart scale. One point of the dividers is placed on the scale where it intersects the fixed line of latitude, the other either above or below, depending on where the required fix lies. The latitude can then be read from the scale. The same procedure is followed on the top or bottom scale for longitude.

Extracting and plotting fixes on charts is a very simple procedure, but it does take time to grasp the basic principle. Always check and double-check every co-ordinate until you are proficient with the technique. A common mistake is failing to appreciate the east–west divide at Greenwich. The time to practise is in the comfort of your home, not out on the water.

Bearings and courses

The route taken between any two points at sea is known as the course, which is also the term used to define the boat's present heading at sea. A bearing is the angle from one position to another relative to true north. It is used to fix or plot positions at sea. Bearings and courses are plotted on charts using 360-degree notation.

Small boats invariably rely on a magnetic compass to indicate courses and bearings. Compasses indicate magnetic north and are subject to several errors.

Positions between points on an Admiralty chart are printed relative to true north, not magnetic north, hence only true tracks should be pencilled on to a chart.

The errors for which a magnetic compass needs to be compensated are deviation and variation. Before an accurate course or bearing can be plotted on a chart these errors have to be allowed for. Likewise, if a course between two points is extracted in true notation off the chart, it will have to be converted into a magnetic reading before a compass course can be steered.

Deviation is an error created by magnetic influences found on the boat itself. Metallic objects, electronic equipment and electrical wiring can all affect compass readings. Determining this error accurately is a skilled and expensive job. The easiest solution is to mount the compass well away from all likely needle-distorting objects. Watch it carefully when the engine is started or when the lights and electronics are switched on. If there is any significant magnetic field then the needle will move, so it will be advisable to fit the compass elsewhere.

Variation is an error created by the earth's own magnetic field. The exact amount varies considerably from place to place and changes at an annual rate. The amount of variation at a point can be found on a chart. Variation is given as being either east or west and is printed inside the compass rose on the chart, or, on some charts, as a series of contour-type lines.

When buying a compass you certainly only get what you pay for. Don't expect accuracy to within a fraction of one degree if the compass only cost you £30. A top-quality magnetic compass is an expensive instrument. Electronic compasses are now available, and these are undoubtedly the way forward for small boat navigation.

Having recognized these errors we now have to compensate for them, and this is where a degree of realism has to be accepted. Most private angling boats are fitted with a compass that is, at best, of a reasonable quality. Steering a 16-ft boat to within a couple of degrees either side of a specific course heading over long distances is in itself no simple task. Allowing for the fact that an accurate deviation reading can often not be determined, there is no point in trying to go over the top converting a magnetic course to a compass course using the precise methods required for high accuracy.

Most dinghy anglers set off from just one or two starting points, rarely venturing further than five miles offshore. Usually they fish maybe a dozen or so marks throughout the year. Once they have located these marks the magnetic course can be noted, and should be the same each and every time that they visit that mark. The errors given above can for the most part then be considered as constant.

Anyone fishing long-range trips should have the back-up of GPS or Decca and would be well advised to enrol on a course of coastal navigation as soon as possible. As travel distances increase, the requirement for a higher degree of accuracy also increases. There are more practical ways of establishing the combined errors of variation and deviation, by establishing the combined error with the use of transit bearings.

Transit bearings are the most accurate method of fixing positions when within sight of land. They have been used by anglers for years for fixing positions and recording marks at sea. To take a transit, two distinctive landmarks that are illustrated on a chart are lined up from the boat at sea. A line is then plotted on to

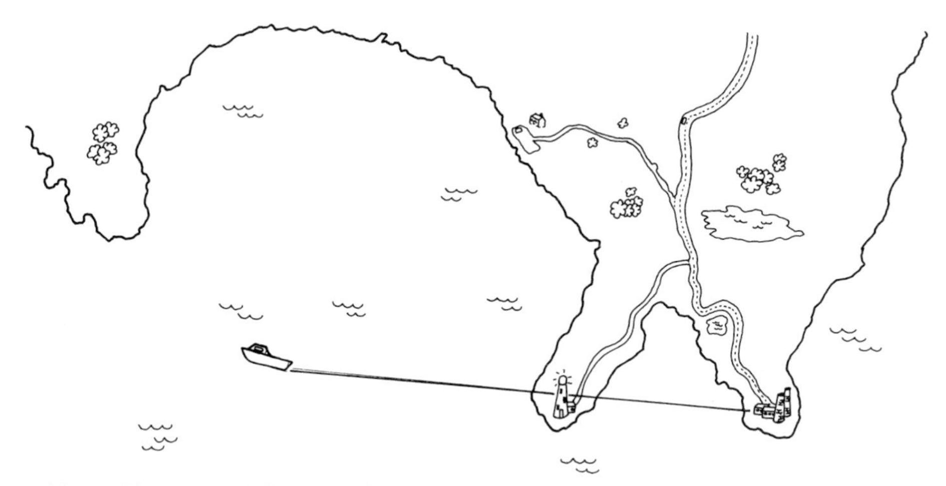

Additional bearings will be required to obtain a 'fix'

Fig. 13 Method of obtaining a boat's position using transit bearings.

a chart, running through both positions. The navigator will know that without any doubt the boat is somewhere along that position line.

The true bearing of the transit is then read off the chart compass rose and compared against the magnetic bearing of the two marks when in transit, viewed from the boat. The difference between the true bearing and the compass reading gives a combined error to work with.

When selecting marks to line up in transit, always select fixed marks. Do not use floating buoys or similar objects which can move over the years and give different readings depending on the size and direction of the tide. Long slim marks such as lighthouses, church spires, factory chimneys, or the right- or left-hand edge of a distinctive rock or headland are excellent choices (Fig. 13).

Carry a small notebook and permanently record as many transit fixes as possible, together with compass courses and running times to and from your regular fishing marks. In the event of fog you will then be able to return home safely by steering a known compass course.

Using more than one transit bearing to establish an accurate fix will rarely be possible, but one transit bearing is always better than none. More often than not precise mark location will depend on steering a compass course for a given distance and from a known starting point, until the transit fix comes into line. If this can then be confirmed with a second bearing off a landmark or another transit, the accuracy will be that much greater.

Any position should always be confirmed using at least three position lines, either compass bearings or transits (Fig. 14). As the distance offshore increases and compass course distances get longer, the degree of accuracy will fall. A hand-held bearing compass is far more accurate for taking bearings than using a fixed steering compass.

Bearings and courses are plotted on to charts using a set of parallel rulers and either the compass rose printed on the chart, or the graduated scale printed on the rulers. The novice should find that using the compass rose is the easiest, though the scale on the rulers offers by far the most accurate way of plotting a bearing or course. The compass rose has two scales, the outer or true scale, and an inner magnetic scale. The magnetic scale has already allowed for the magnetic

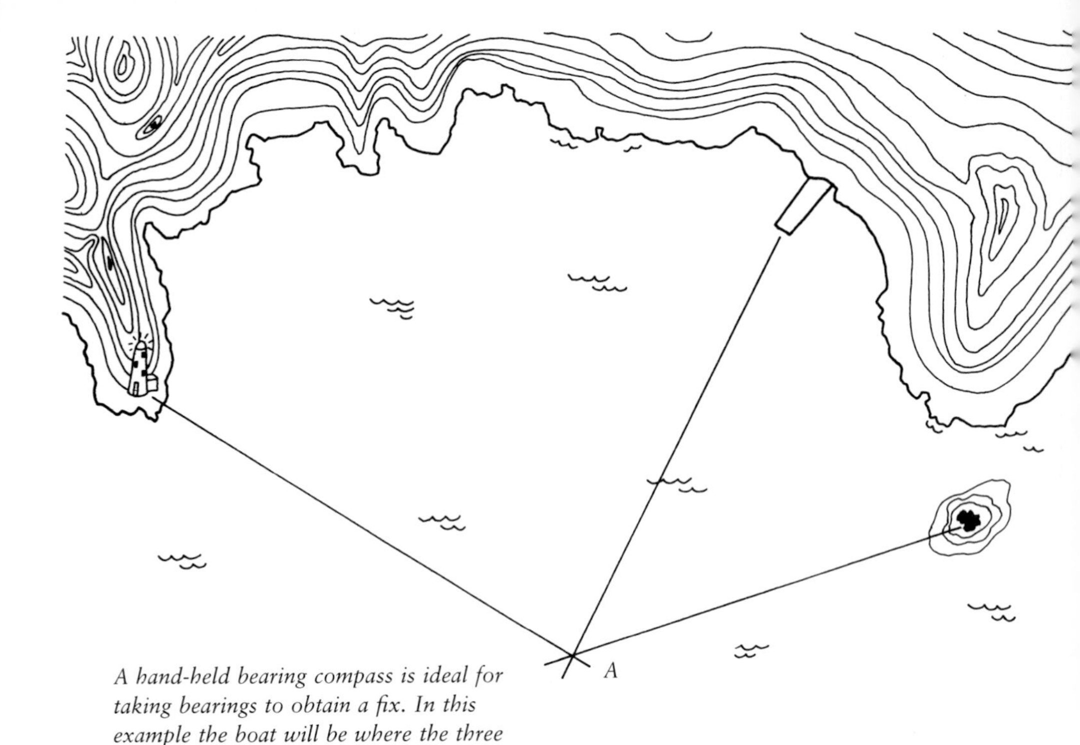

A hand-held bearing compass is ideal for taking bearings to obtain a fix. In this example the boat will be where the three bearings cross at position A

Fig. 14 Method of fixing a boat's position using three compass bearings.

variation in the area covered by the chart at the time of publication, with the annual increase or decrease given.

To plot or extract the course between two points, lay the outer edge of the rulers between those two points, then very carefully transpose the rulers across to the nearest compass rose until the leading edge lies through the centre spot of the rose. The bearing can then be read taking care to choose the scale relevant to the direction heading, i.e. bearing 90 degrees, and not 270 degrees. A return route can easily be calculated by either adding or subtracting 180 degrees. To plot a given course, reverse this procedure. Always use a compass rose as close as possible to the working area on the chart to minimize errors caused by moving the rulers over a wide expanse of chart.

Reading a chart

A wealth of information is found on an Admiralty chart, which is both useful and essential from both a safety and a practical point of view. Amongst other things, it is important for the dinghy angler fully to understand the system of buoyage. Various types of buoys are used in inshore waters throughout the world as an aid to inshore navigation. They indicate to shipping safe routes to follow, while highlighting any isolated dangers and designated shipping lanes. The UK has adopted the International Association of Lighthouse Authorities (IALA) system A, which is the system printed on all UK charts (Fig. 15).

The system consists of several types of buoy, each used specifically to indicate a certain type of navigational hazard, feature or a buoyed channel. Channels leading toward ports and harbours will be indicated by port-hand and

Fig. 15 (*opposite*) Buoyage.

Lateral marks
Used generally to mark the sides of well-defined navigable channels

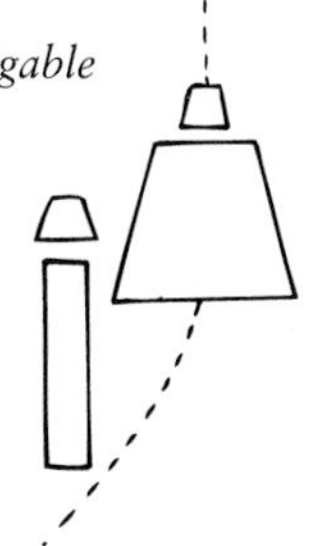

Navigable channel

Direction of buoyage

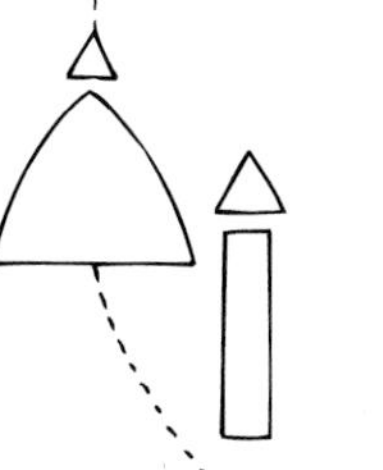

Port-hand marks
Light:
colour – red
rhythm – any

Starboard-hand marks
Light:
colour – green
rhythm – any

Cardinal marks
Used to indicate the direction from the mark in which the best navigable water lies, or to draw attention to a bend, junction or fork in a channel, or to mark the end of a shoal.
Lights: always white

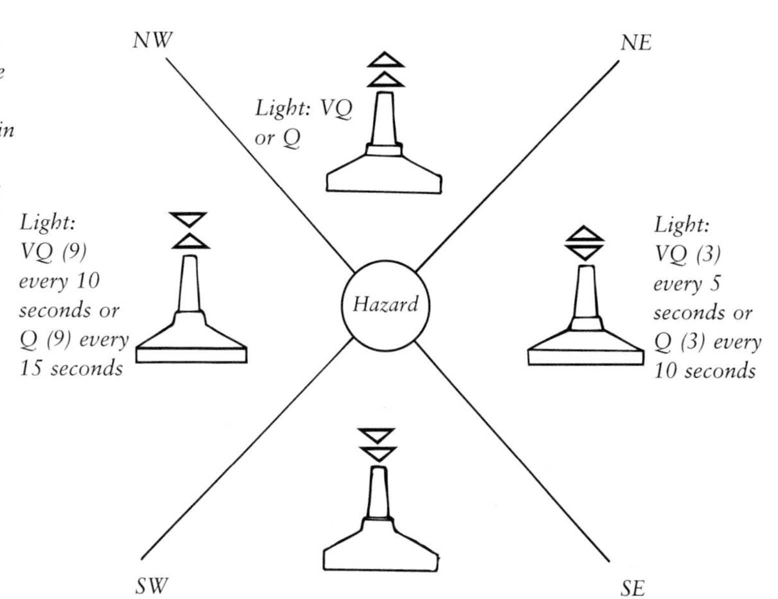

Light: VQ (6) + LFl every 10 seconds or Q (6) + LFl every 15 seconds

Other marks

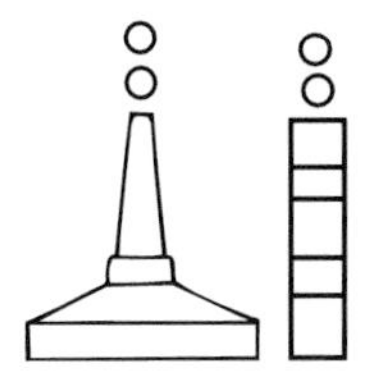

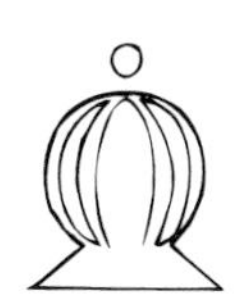

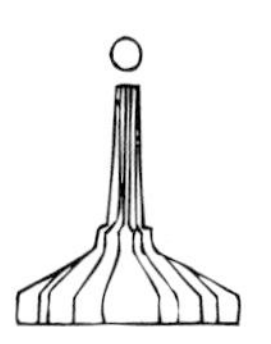

Isolated danger marks – black and red
Use: to mark a small isolated danger with navigable water all round
Light:
colour – white
rhythm – group flashing (2)

Safe water marks – red and white
Use: mid-channel or landfall
Light:
colour – white
rhythm – isophase occulting or 1 long flash every 10 seconds

Special marks – yellow
Any shape not conflicting with lateral or safe water marks
Light:
colour – yellow
rhythm – different from other white lights used on buoys

starboard-hand buoys. The port-hand buoys, coloured red, are either can-shape or a pillar or a spar buoy. Starboard-hand buoys are green, either conical or, again, a pillar or spar buoy. The lights on each are coloured red and green respectively, with a flashing light sequence at night, ranging from set groups of a certain sequence to continual very quick flashing light.

This information is found on the chart adjacent to the buoy, e.g. QKFLG denotes a starboard-hand buoy with a single long green flash every five seconds. GpF1(2)R indicates a port-hand buoy flashing in distinctive groups consisting of two red flashes.

Apart from showing the safe route into a harbour, buoyed channels can also help to indicate useful marks to the angler. A deep channel running through an otherwise shallow area will almost certainly attract fish and should be worth exploring. Many vessels using the channel will be restricted by their draft and an angler should never anchor in the middle of a shipping lane. In some circumstances it might be possible to anchor and fish on the edge of the channel, or to fish at low water when commercial or other traffic is not around.

Buoys known as cardinal marks are used to indicate specific hazards to navigation, usually sandbanks, shallow water reefs and shoals, more useful fishing marks! There are four types of cardinal marks which correspond to the four points of the compass, i.e. north, south, east and west. From a navigational point of view the buoys indicate the side of that hazard on which it is safe to pass.

For example, a north cardinal buoy could be used to indicate the northern edge of a sandbank, so it would be safe to pass north of the buoy. A south cardinal buoy, placed on the southern edge of a reef, would indicate it was safe to pass south of the buoy.

Cardinal buoys are pillars or spars, with topmarks fitted, consisting of two black cones. On a north cardinal buoy the points of both cones point upwards, on a south cardinal buoy they both point downwards. A west cardinal buoy has the cones fitted with their points together, resembling a wine glass (remember W for wine). The east cardinal buoy has the bases of the two cones together. Cardinal buoys are coloured black and yellow with the cones pointing towards the black sector, so on a north buoy the black is at the top, on a west buoy the black is in the middle, and so on.

Lights on cardinal buoys are white and are either very quick flashing or quick flashing. To help remember the light sequences on cardinal buoys, think of a compass as a clock face. The east cardinal buoy indicates three o'clock, and has a sequence of three flashes, e.g. VQkF1(3)5s; very quick flash three times every five seconds. West represents nine o'clock, and the lights are in a sequence of nine, e.g. QkF1(9)15s or quick flash nine every 15 seconds. The south cardinal buoy has a sequence of six, plus the long flash. The north buoy has either a quick flash or a very quick flash sequence. Of all types of buoyage, cardinal buoys probably offer the boat angler the strongest indication of a useful mark.

Isolated danger marks are also useful for pointing the boat angler towards a few fish. An isolated danger mark is erected or moored on or above an isolated danger of limited extent, which has navigable water all around it. It could be used to indicate a small and prominent bank which is well offshore, or perhaps a pinnacle of rock, again standing out in otherwise safe water; both are excellent fish-holding areas.

Isolated danger marks are black with one or more red horizontal bands. The buoy itself will be a pillar or a spar, with a black double-sphere topmark. The light sequence on this type of buoy consists of a group of two flashes. The association of two flashes and two spheres in the topmark help one to remember the characteristics of this marker.

A safe water mark is used to indicate there is navigable water all around the mark. It is usually used as a centreline, mid-channel or landfall buoy. Safe water buoys are coloured with red and white vertical stripes, which distinguish them from the black-banded danger-marking buoys. The buoy itself may be either spherical or a pillar/spar shape, with a single red sphere as a topmark which is only fitted if the buoy is the pillar/spar type. Safe water buoys are not buoys likely to convey a great deal of information to the angler, but are worth using as a reference mark, or perhaps as a way point when heading further offshore.

The last common type of buoy found in inshore waters is the yellow-coloured special mark buoy, used to indicate to the mariner a special area or feature. Typical applications for the special mark buoy are to indicate traffic separation zones, military exercise zones, cable or pipeline marks, and, of particular interest to anglers, outfall pipes or spoil/dumping ground; both of which attract certain species of fish.

As mentioned above, yellow is the colour used for special mark buoys, but the actual shape is optional, but must not conflict with the shape of other buoys in the area. The top mark, if fitted, takes the form of a single yellow X. A yellow light is used, with any rhythm other than that used for the white lights of cardinal, isolated danger and safe water buoys. It is essential that all boat users are familiar with all types of buoyage.

Apart from a knowledge of buoyage, you should learn how to interpret the wealth of other information readily available from charts. Obviously charts give an accurate indication about the actual depths of water in an area. But a surprisingly large proportion of boat anglers fall to realize they also show the type of seabed.

Abbreviations are used to denote whether or not the seabed consists of sand, shingle, mud, rock, etc. This should help the angler work out which species of fish will be present in that area, depending on the location and time of the year.

For example, the chart might indicate a sand bank consists of shingle, indicated by Sh, which, when fishing in the south west, might suggest the presence of turbot and brill. An adjacent bank might consist of sand, indicated by S, which might suggest a population of plaice and small-eyed rays. Areas of mud, denoted with a capital M, could suggest thornback rays or perhaps sole.

The Admiralty produces a booklet which gives all of the abbreviations on the charts, including an explanation of the light sequences, etc., detailed in the first part of this chapter. The booklet, ref. no. 5011, is available from good chandlers or any Admiralty Hydrographic department. If you wish to obtain a copy, phone 01272 29229 or 01278 426759.

Modern Admiralty charts are printed in four prominent colours. Land above, mean high water springs (MHWS), is coloured a sandy yellow. The foreshore between MHWS and MLWS, mean low water springs, is coloured green, and all water between MLWS and the 5 m

(5 yd) sounding line is coloured sky blue. The 10 m (10yd) line is also indicated on some large detail charts with a blue line. This in itself provides a lot of useful information for the boat angler, as a lot of fish will concentrate at times just below the MLWS mark.

Depths and heights printed on an Admiralty chart are in metres. Underlined figures within an estuary are drying heights in metres and centimetres above chart data, which is approximately the level of the lowest astronomical tide, or MLWS. All other heights are taken as being above MHWS, mean high water spring, or their minimum height above sea level at any one time.

Tide rips of headlands are other noted fish-holding areas. Predators such as bass and pollack love to hunt in fast water, lying in wait for unsuspecting bait fish to be carried helplessly towards them. Charts indicate tide races by a series of ripples. The times when these tide races are at their strongest will vary considerably from place to place. I would always advise extreme caution when attempting to fish anywhere near a tide race in a small boat, especially at times of peak tidal flow or when the wind is in the opposite direction to the flow of water.

The locations of all known wrecks are also given but these are rarely completely accurate. More detailed positions, plus the location of other wrecks within the area, can be obtained by requesting a search from the Admiralty Hydrographic Office in Taunton, Tel: 01823 337900. For a minimal fee precise latitude and longitude co-ordinates of all known wrecks within a given area can be obtained.

From a navigational point of view the other important information printed on a chart refers to all relevant tidal details. Tidal diamonds are located at various positions on the chart and referred to in a table elsewhere. These tidal diamonds are fixed where tidal streams have been analysed over a period of time. The average results are given in the table.

The diamonds allow you to calculate the direction and the strength of the tidal streams at different times during the tidal cycle. Obviously, these are points which must be considered when planning any long-haul trip, as it is only by knowing the rate and direction of the tide that allowances can be made to the course. This is essential when navigating in restricted visibility or out of sight of land.

5 Launching

Launching from a beach

Launching a boat from a sandy beach is rarely without risk if you have to drive your vehicle on to the sand. All too often things go wrong, and problems, which initially start as minor hiccups, can escalate out of all proportion. When the tide is flooding, the end result can be the loss of your towing vehicle.

The golden rule of beach launching is to get to know the beach before you attempt to drive on to it. Usually this will entail little more than chatting to local anglers, followed by a close inspection of the launch site at low water. Look for small isolated patches of rock which can damage a hull. Streams running across the sand are best avoided, as there will probably be patches of soft sand in the vicinity into which the trailer or car may sink. Areas of mud should also be avoided.

A lot of beaches which are regular launch sites have resident tractors, used for launching and retrieving boats. These are usually owned and operated by local dinghy angling clubs but for a nominal charge they will usually launch non-club boats. The advantage in using a tractor to launch a boat is that it is often possible to launch and retrieve without uncoupling the trailer from the tractor, thus avoiding a lot of hard physical work, and mess in your car.

Many private boat owners, however, will have to use the family car to launch their boat. There are an increasing number of cars on the road with four-

Unless you follow a few basic rules when launching on flat, sandy beaches, this can be the result!

wheel drive. These are ideal for anyone who regularly launches off a beach. But, with a little care, two-wheel drive vehicles can cope with most beaches.

Always ensure your car is in a reasonable condition before venturing on to the beach. Attempting to drive on sand with tyres bordering on the illegal tread limit or with an unreliable starter motor is inviting disaster. I can even remember one incident when a car which had run out of petrol had to be towed off a beach!

The safest time to drive on to any beach is when the tide is on its way out. Then, if things do go wrong, time will be on your side. The worst time is at low water on a spring-tide. The beach at low water on these bigger-than-average tides is often very soft, usually with a high mud content. Not only is the chance of running into difficulties higher, but you will have a lot less time to get out of trouble. The tide waits for no one, and if you get stuck on the flattest part of the beach, water will be lapping around the seats in minutes.

Careful planning is the way to avoid using the beach at the wrong times. Launching the boat is usually a lot quicker than retrieving and is less likely to lead to problems. On the other hand,

A tractor is the safest way to launch from a sandy beach; many dinghy angling clubs now own their own tractors.

winching a boat and engine on to a trailer in the surf will all too often result in the trailer tyres getting bogged down to the axles. When the tide is ebbing, it is simply a case of waiting for the water to drop past the trailer. Then drop the car back and couple the trailer to the ball hitch. When the tide is flooding, you will have to use your car to pull the trailer out with a rope.

The safest procedure to follow for both launching and retrieving is as follows. Always do as much preparation as possible prior to launching and before you drive on to the sand. This keeps the time your car will be at risk to an absolute minimum. Jobs like removing securing straps and trailer lights take time. These are the sort of jobs which should be carried out on firm ground with no risk of tyres sinking.

When the tide is ebbing it will be safe to drive to the water's edge, uncouple the trailer, launch the boat, then remove the car and trailer to safety. On the other hand, if the tide is flooding you should

The safest way to launch from a sandy beach is to park the car clear of the water's edge and either manhandle the boat the last few yards or wait for the tide to float the boat off.

park about ten yards clear of the water's edge, more on very flat beaches. Having uncoupled the trailer, move the car further up the beach while you launch the boat. Parking the car's drive wheels on flat boards will prevent them sinking.

With very heavy boats it might be easier to drop the trailer quickly at the water's edge, then park further up the beach. Get a friend to uncouple the trailer so you can stay with the car, if necessary, keeping it moving forward very slowly to prevent the tyres from sinking.

Retrieving the boat is more time-consuming and with an increased risk of running into problems. Once again, when the tide is ebbing, it will be safe to venture right to the water's edge with your car, unless low water is near. Uncouple the trailer and pull it to the boat. Winch the boat on to the trailer and, depending on the size of your outfit, either pull it out of the water to the car or wait for the water to ebb past the trailer coupling so the car can be backed down to the trailer.

When the tide is flooding, you will have to exercise a lot more caution. Drive the car to about 20 yds from the water's edge and park with the drive wheels on flat boards, uncouple and pull the trailer to the boat. Winch the boat back on to the trailer then, if your boat is light enough and the trailer wheels have not sunk into the sand, pull the boat and trailer to the car.

It is common when winching the boat back on to the trailer for the extra weight to drive the trailer wheels down into the sand. Attempting to free these by hand is usually futile. The only way that you will pull the trailer out is with a rope and by using the car.

At the first indication of trouble a rope should be tied to the trailer and led out of the water on to dry sand. The car is then backed down to the rope, which is then tied to the car ball hitch. Driving off at a slight angle to the trailer will usually pull the trailer free. At the slightest hint of the car's wheels spinning under the heavy load, stop, reverse, and try again, following a different line and at an increased angle.

Pulling at an angle as opposed to

pulling in a straight line will lift one trailer wheel out at a time, which is easier than struggling to pull both wheels free at the same time. As soon as the trailer is moving, slowly pull it well clear of the water line. Then untie the rope, back the car down to the trailer, recouple it and drive it off the beach to safety.

If at any time during these procedures the car drive wheels get bogged down, it is vital you direct all of your attentions to freeing the car. The boat can always be relaunched and anchored and at worst you will have to wait a few hours to retrieve your trailer. Nothing is worse than losing your car to the tide.

Never panic and frantically try to drive the wheels out. All this will achieve is sinking the car further down to the axles, drastically worsening the situation. Raise the alarm and grab as many helpers from the beach as you can and, ideally, the assistance of another vehicle.

If the water is a fair way from the car, a couple of men should be able to lift the wheels free. But if water is lapping around the wheels, tie the longest rope you can find to the car, usually an anchor rope, and make every effort to get help from another vehicle. Once again, pulling at an angle is more likely to free badly bogged-down wheels. Pushing rubber car mats or pebbles beneath the trapped wheels can sometimes give the required traction to drive the car free from the hole.

Launching from concrete slips

Launching a trailerable boat from a concrete slip is normally a lot easier than launching the same boat from a sand or shingle beach. With few exceptions, the basic procedure is to reverse the trailer down the slip, unclip the boat and push it free. Retrieving the boat at the end of the day is more or less the reverse of the above procedure. Yet every weekend lots of anglers who trail their boats run into difficulties launching from slips.

Reversing a trailer when you are not used to it is difficult. In order to reverse any trailer with a degree of proficiency you must practise beforehand. The time to practise reversing your boat trailer around tight bends is not on a Bank Holiday Monday at high tide, when just about every launch site in the country will be heavily congested. As soon as you acquire a boat, tow it to a quiet car park and, with the help of a friend, practise reversing around both left-hand and right-hand corners. The basic reversing procedure with a trailer attached is to turn the car steering wheel the opposite way to the direction you are trying to reverse the trailer. After a couple of hours' practice it should come as second nature.

Always ensure you get someone to watch your back, so as to prevent damaging your boat or possibly injuring someone. The other golden rule of reversing is that if you start to go wrong and the trailer starts to jack-knife, stop, pull forward, and have a second or third attempt.

It is bad policy to arrive at a slipway, only usable at certain states of the tide, with about half an hour to spare before the water ebbs past the bottom of the slip. Arrive with plenty of time to spare and you will not end up frantically rushing to get into the water before the tide ebbs past the bottom of the slip. Rushing is a guaranteed way to cause problems.

The times when a slip can be used for launching vary greatly from one part of the country to another. A good concrete slip which can be used 24 hours a day on all heights of tide is rare. Few are usable even five hours either side of high water. Slips with plenty of water for only three hours or less either side of high water are the norm. Remember, if a slip is usable three hours either side of high water on neap tides, then at best it will be usable two and a half hours either side of high tide on spring tides.

If you calculate there will be enough water to launch your boat three and a half hours before high water, be ready to launch about four hours before. Then as soon as there is enough depth of water available you can launch your boat. And if there are other boats waiting to launch you will not lose too much fishing time.

Having launched three and a half hours before high water, you will roughly be able to retrieve your boat up to three and a half hours after high water. Aim to get back to the slip no later than two and a half hours after high water. Giving yourself an hour's leeway makes sense in case you are delayed. Leave it to the last minute, and it will be likely others will have the same idea. The last thing you want is to arrive back at the slip with minutes to spare before the water has gone, only to find a couple of boats waiting in front of you to retrieve.

Always ensure you connect and prime fuel lines, have the anchor and lifejackets ready for immediate use, before you launch. Don't forget to secure the drain cock in the stern of the boat. Attach a line to the bow of the boat long enough for you to hang on to as the boat comes off the trailer.

Leave the winch cable attached to the bow of the boat to prevent the boat running off the trailer when you back down the slip. This is especially important when using roller-coaster-type trailers from which the boat can easily slide if jolted. Always reverse the trailer slowly down the slip. Most slips will have a fair amount of seaweed and algae growing on them. Apply the car brakes too hard and you will skid.

Chock at least one of the car's rear wheels before launching or retrieving a boat; large pebbles or rocks are better than nothing. The car's handbrake might be adequate for normal driving purposes, but working on slips with a heavy boat and trailer is very different. Select a forward gear for additional security if parking a car and trailer on a slip.

On a perfect slip it is possible to launch and retrieve your boat without immersing the wheel bearings. But all too often the trailer will have to be backed right into the water in order to give sufficient depth to prevent scratching the boat and putting additional strain on to the trailer winch. If the bearings get wet then they will require servicing (see Chapter 6).

The procedure for retrieving the boat is more or less the reverse of launching. Some boats are awkward to stow back on their trailers, due to poor trailer design. As a general rule immersing the trailer to about the second roller is about right, depending on the angle of the slip and design of your boat. Practice will show you what works best for your outfit.

Driving a two-wheel-drive car back up a steep and slippery slip can cause problems, and the various methods for dealing with this situation are covered next.

If other anglers are waiting to use a slip it is polite to get out of their way as soon as possible. If the slip is wide enough for two or three boats at a time, keep to one side and do not launch or retrieve in the middle. If you are experiencing problems don't be afraid to ask for help or advice, which will invariably be freely given.

Launching from a steep slip

Around the country there are many excellent slips, on which the average family four-door car can easily cope with launching a typical 16-ft rig. But there are many where four-wheel drive is a far safer bet, and others where even a four-wheel drive will struggle. However, with a little bit of thought, there is a method that allows even a typical family saloon to be utilized in safely launching and retrieving a boat on most concrete slips.

The biggest problem facing boat owners who tow their boats today is front-wheel drive. A growing number of front-wheel-drive vehicles are on the roads today because they provide better road handling. But front-wheel drive is vastly inferior to the traditional rear-wheel drive when a car is required to launch a boat. The problem is traction, or lack of traction.

When a trailer is coupled to a ball hitch, the weight on the front end of the vehicle is reduced. If that vehicle has front-wheel drive, then the amount of traction on the front tyres is reduced. Back a car with a heavy trailer down a sloping slip and the problem is exaggerated further, with even more weight being applied to the back wheels and a further reduction in load on the front end. When trying to pull a boat up the slip the result is wheel spinning, or, worse still, total loss of traction resulting in the entire rig sliding uncontrollably backwards into the water.

Rear-wheel drive is far more reliable, with traction actually increased when a boat is attached. Four-wheel drive is better still, but there are plenty of slips where even four-wheel drive will struggle. Thankfully it is often possible to launch and retrieve a boat safely using your own car, simply by utilizing a rope to lower the boat into the water and then to haul it out again.

You will need a sufficient length of strong rope. Use cheap rope and you run the risk of it snapping, with obvious and often disastrous consequences. Avoid using your anchor warp unless you have to. You do not want to get expensive anchor warp covered in grease or chafed by friction.

You will also need at least two good wheel chocks. The handbrake should always be applied and the car left in gear, but wheel chocks provide essential extra security on steep and slippery surfaces.

When the boat is ready for the sea, with bow line attached, it is positioned as close to the water as the towing vehicle can safely take it. One end of the launch rope is then securely attached to the winch post of the trailer and a wheel chock jammed under one of the trailer tyres; a second chock is placed under one of the rear wheels of the car.

Uncouple the trailer, taking great care to ensure it does not move backwards, and take at least two turns around the ball hitch with the launch rope. When everything is ready, remove the chocks from the trailer tyres, ensuring someone is taking the strain on the launch rope.

The trailer can now be gently lowered into the water by carefully feeding the launch rope around the ball hitch. Always ensure you take two full turns around the ball hitch – with less it is possible for a heavy boat to run backwards out of control. It is advisable for the person who is holding the rope to wear a pair of gloves to prevent rope burns and also to improve the grip on the rope. When the boat is slipped off its trailer, the trailer can either be manhandled back to the car or simply pulled up to level ground using the car.

Retrieving the boat is straightforward. The car is again taken as close to the water as it can go, the wheels chocked, and rope attached to the trailer. The trailer is lowered down towards the boat, and the launch rope securely tied to the car ball hitch. The boat is winched on to the trailer, and then towed up the slip.

Doglegged slips are a more awkward situation. The problem arises in getting everything into position but often doglegged slips have a steel ring cemented into the harbour wall for just such purposes.

The boat is again positioned as close to the water as the car can safely take it, and trailer wheels chocked. Before you commence the launch procedure it may be necessary to park at the top end of the dogleg and manoeuvre the trailer around the bend using chocks and rope. The launch rope is fed through the steel ring before attaching it to the car.

There are two ways that the trailer can be lowered into the water. Either the launch rope can be allowed to slip around the ball hitch as before, or, in certain situations, the boat and trailer can be gently backed down the slip by reversing the car with launch rope attached to the ball hitch. If there is no ring or similar fitting which can be utilized, careful manipulation and logical use of chocks, rope and vehicle will nearly always get you afloat. Try and get local advice first; in a lot of areas there may even be a pair of helping hands for the cost of a pint or two!

Launching on a steep and very slippery slip. Note how the towing vehicle has been positioned well above the worst of the weed growths.

6 Maintenance

Boats

Boat maintenance should follow a more or less constant programme of cleaning and servicing but, in all honesty, modern GRP boats require little maintenance other than a thorough wash down after use. That said, months of regular use will invariably have taken their toll on most boats, and the end of the season is generally a good time of the year to give the boat a good going over. If, like many anglers, you fish throughout the year, then the end of summer is still a good time to service your boat, for reasons that will become apparent in this section.

Unfortunately we cannot all enjoy the luxury of overwintering our boats under cover. Most boats are kept out of doors and most of us will have to work on them out of doors at a time of the year when the weather is, at best, unpredictable. Wait for a decent break in the weather before starting work; struggling against the elements is not the best way to locate and rectify defects.

Always ensure your boat's cockpit is covered throughout the cold months. If you do not have a purpose-made cockpit cover then improvise by using a large sheet of canvas or plastic. Frost can cause serious damage to a fibreglass hull when water, which has been absorbed into small cracks or gaps, expands as it freezes. I have seen one hull that was split almost in two by frozen water trapped between decks.

The best way to start any thorough overhaul is to strip everything off the boat. Completely empty all stowage lockers, removing as much ancillary equipment as you can. Then start with as close to a bare hull as possible. A good scrub down with hot soapy water is the first step, followed by rinsing off in fresh water.

If the boat has been kept on a mooring throughout the season there will surely be a lot of weed growth on the hull below the waterline, which will have to be removed. Not only will the boat's overall performance be greatly affected by a heavy growth of weed on the hull, but any cracks or chips on the hull, which must receive attention, will be hidden. Some boat yards have high-pressure jet washers to remove weed but the majority of us will be forced to tackle the job with a scrubbing brush, although there are chemical preparations available to help.

Stubborn grease stains or marks on the gel coat can be removed with a non-abrasive scouring bathroom-type cleaner or any of the purpose-made marine preparations. Some of the abrasive domestic cleaners will scratch the gloss finish off the gel coat, resulting in areas of damage which are more prone to harbouring weed growths and discoloration.

While you are cleaning the hull, note any cracks or chips in the gel coat, or areas where the laminate or bonding between any two mouldings appears to have weakened. A water-based felt-tipped pen can be used to highlight these for future attention and can be easily washed off when the repairs have been carried out.

Outboard, areas of the gel coat which tend to get damaged most frequently are around the base edge of the transom, along and adjacent to the keel and the bow area. Knocking chunks out of the gel coat is almost a fact of life for anyone who trailers their boat, with most damage occurring when launching and retrieving. In the short term most of these are of little consequence unless excessively deep, when water is allowed to penetrate into the glass matting beneath, but, in the long term, all damage will lead to more serious problems if not attended to. If the boat is kept on a mooring any damage, no matter how minor, should be repaired at once.

All chandlers sell both gel coat and fibreglass repair kits. These consist of a quantity of gel coat, hardener, matting and instructions. Getting an exact colour match with a standard gel coat kit can prove difficult, but many of the better boat manufacturers will supply, at low cost, a kit which gives as close to the original colour match as possible. Follow all instructions to the letter.

A serious case of neglect. Not only will weed growing on the hull affect the boat's performance, it will also hide any damage to the gel coat

Forget any attempt of fibreglassing or gel coat repairs on cold damp days; wait for dry warmish weather for the best results. The same advice applies for more extensive repairs involving the actual structure. Thorough preparation is the key to a good repair.

When inspecting the hull, ensure the keel band and bilge runner bands, if fitted, are secure. The heads of the securing screws tend to snap off, which will, firstly, result in a loose band and, secondly, allow water to soak into the hull fabric from around the damaged screw head. Damaged screws will either have to be drilled out and replaced with slightly larger self-tapping screws, or sealed over with sealer or gel coat and new screws fitted elsewhere. All fittings, which are either screwed or bolted into the hull both above and below the waterline, should be fitted on to a sealing bed of a quality marine silicone sealant to prevent water ingress.

Most modern fibreglass hulls have at least one drain plug fitted into the stern. I have found, over a period of time, that these can start to leak. They only cost a couple of pounds to replace and it is a good idea to replace them if there are any signs that they are losing their efficiency. Ensure a good squirt of marine-grade sealant around the edges. Always use quality stainless steel, self-tapping screws intended for below waterline use for hull fixings, and not alloy rivets, mild steel or inferior-grade stainless steel which quickly corrode (Fig. 16).

Inboard, depending on how much use your boat has had, the deck might require repainting. A lot of good, hardwearing, marine deck paints are available from all

Drain cocks do wear out and leak. Replace, using stainless steel screws and a quality marine sealant.

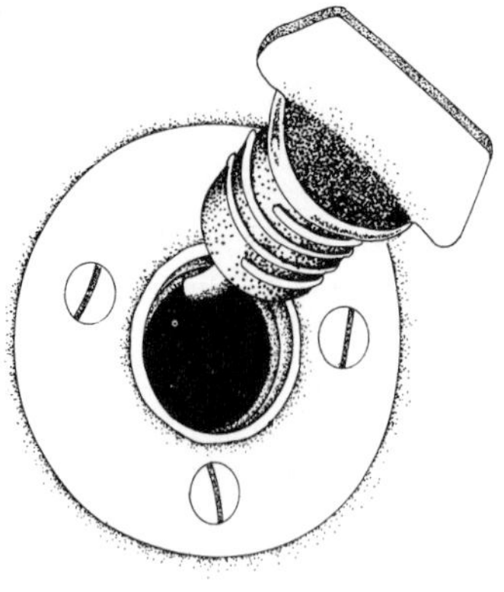

Fig. 16 Standard drain cock fitted in the transom of most dinghies.

chandlers. They are well worth the extra purchase cost to give your boat's deck protection from knocks and give you a safe non-slip surface from which to fish.

Now is a good time to check the condition of every connection and wire throughout the complete electrical circuit. If there is any indication of dampness or corrosion then the joints should be dried off and cleaned with a fine piece of sandpaper to ensure a sound connection. Dismantle the fuse box or distribution panel and look for signs of damp and corrosion, and renew all connections where required. One bad connection in the wrong place will play havoc with the boat's entire electrical system.

Check fuel line frequently for signs of wear and paint any scratches before corrosion starts. Never over-fill petrol cans or tanks otherwise they will leak through the vent caps when they are opened

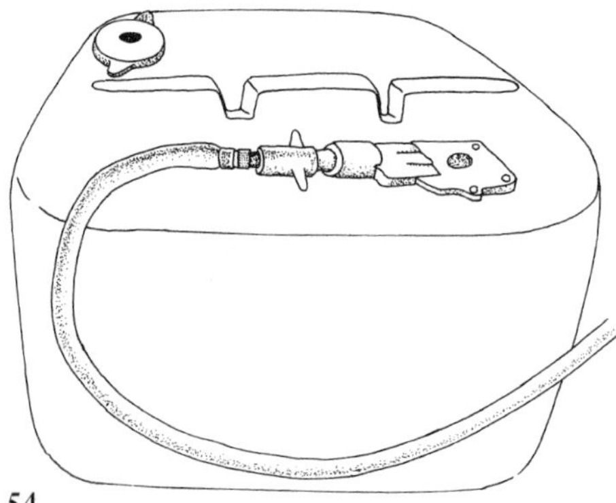

Fixed fuel tanks and fuel delivery lines should also be closely examined for any sign of corrosion, perishing or leakage. I usually renew fuel connections at least once a year. Trimming back and re-connecting flexible fuel lines only takes a few minutes of your time, but can save you a lot of aggravation in the future (Fig. 17).

Give all fixed deck hardwear a good examination, checking all bolts and screws holding cleats, fairleads, bow rollers, and other deck fittings for tightness. If your boat is regularly launched and retrieved from a trailer, pay particular attention to the winching eye on the bow. This receives an incredible amount of very heavy localized stress, and should be examined for any signs of fracturing to the hull where it is fitted.

Items of equipment fitted within the boat such as bilge pumps, transducers and fire extinguishers should all be checked. Most bilge pumps soon develop leaks which are often repairable with service kits, and they often get choked with debris which should be cleaned out. Transducers fitted within the hull can work loose, affecting the efficiency of your fishfinder (Fig. 18).

The best way to approach boat maintenance is slowly but surely. Never try to cut corners or skimp on quality. If you do, then operating a boat in a marine environment will very quickly expose any shortcomings, with the end result often being an even greater bill than if the job was tackled correctly to start with.

Basic outboard engine service

All engines, regardless of how much use they have had, should receive a thorough

Fig. 17 Standard five-gallon outboard engine fuel tank.

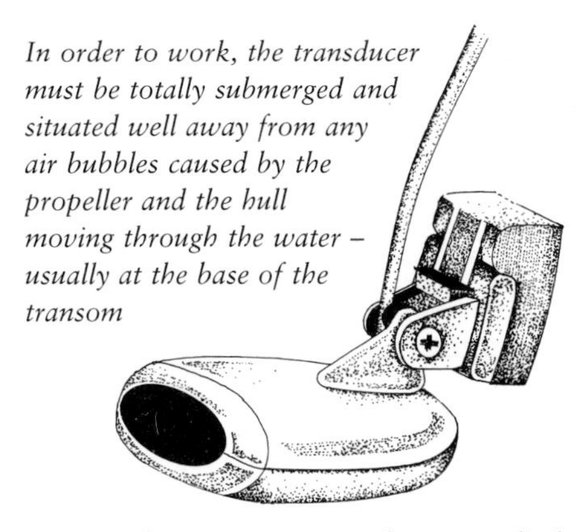

Fig. 18 Skimmer-type transducer supplied with Eagle fishfinders, mounted to the transom of the boat.

service at least once a year, twice a year if they have been used extensively. In addition, prior to any period of lay-up, an engine should be thoroughly examined, flushed with fresh water, drained, and then lubricated where necessary. The procedure for preparing an engine for a winter lay-up is detailed later.

Different engines from different manufacturers vary in design and build, but the sequence of events to follow for a standard service will be much the same. Before you start, a comprehensive workshop guide should be fully consulted. You should ensure you have all the tools and parts you may require, including any specialist tools needed for your engine. If you feel you are not competent to carry out the service yourself, take the engine to a qualified marine mechanic.

The first step is to remove the engine cover, then remove the spark plugs and, using a compression gauge, check the compression in each cylinder, by turning the engine over. The correct compression figures will be found in the engine's handbook. There should not be a difference of more than plus or minus 15psi between any two cylinders. If there is, you have a fault which will probably need the services of a qualified outboard engine mechanic.

Examine the sacrificial anode fitted to your engine. Anodes are designed to corrode away as a result of electrolysis, which is caused by the propeller spinning in salt water. Were an anode not fitted, then the various alloy engine components would be vulnerable and damaged.

Different designs will be found on different engines with some anodes doubling as trim tabs. Anodes are designed to corrode gradually with the effects of electrolysis, sacrificing themselves and thus preventing wear on the engine components (Fig. 19). The majority of external modern engine parts are made from alloys which are extremely vulnerable to the corroding effects of electrolysis. In order to work, anodes should be clean and certainly not painted. If they are anywhere near 50 per cent worn they should be replaced.

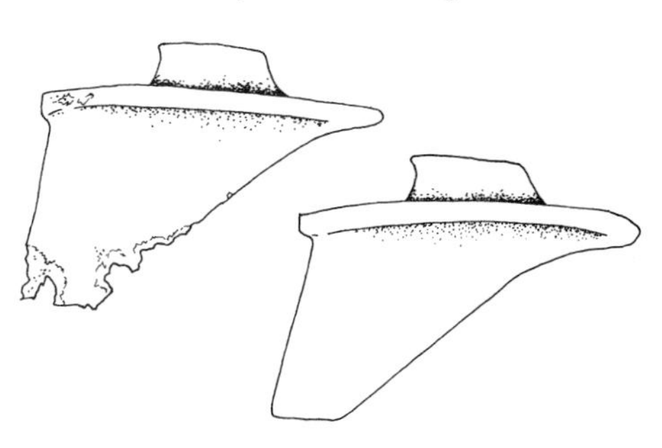

Fig. 19 Sacrificial anodes fitted to cavitation plate on most outboard engines. The one on the left clearly shows the effects of corrosion resulting from electrolysis.

Before removing the lower leg and gearbox in order to get at the drive shaft, waterpump and impeller, place the gear shift into forward. This will make assembly a lot easier and is an essential step on several makes of engine. Having slackened and undone the various bolts and screws, carefully remove the casing and slide the drive shaft free.

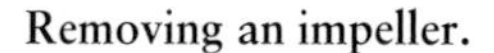

Removing an impeller.

New and old. Note how the vanes on the old impeller, the one at the top, have acquired a permanent set. This will affect the efficiency of the boat's cooling system.

Examine the shaft for any signs of twisting or damage, and replace the rubber seal if it is perished or split. Remove the waterpump and replace the impeller with a new one at least once a year. The efficiency of an impeller deteriorates with use, with obvious effects on the engine's cooling system. Even when the engine has not had much use, it is a wise step to replace the impeller as the efficiency will still deteriorate with time. For the sake of saving money by prolonging the life of the existing impeller, you will be putting your engine at risk of far more serious damage. Where the impeller has a brass insert, ensure that it has not become unbonded from the rubber.

Examine the waterpump insert and faceplate for wear, replacing with new parts as required; also examine the rubber waterpipe seal. Assemble the waterpump using new gaskets, having first checked that all surfaces have been thoroughly cleaned.

Before fitting the new impeller, you should lubricate it and the inside of the waterpump with a light lubricating oil. Place the pump housing on top of the impeller and, by applying gentle downwards pressure, rotate the drive shaft clockwise. This will gently ease the flexible impeller blades into the pump housing without damaging them. Refit the water slinger on top of the pump housing, then slide on the drive shaft seal.

To drain out the old gearbox oil, first remove the top vent screw. Then, with a container in position to catch the oil, remove the bottom drain plug. Check the oil for any sign of milkiness or water. If there are signs that water has entered the gearbox you will have to replace the lower unit seals; once again this would possibly be a job best left to your local dealer.

Some drain plugs are fitted with a thin magnet to catch loose particles of metal.

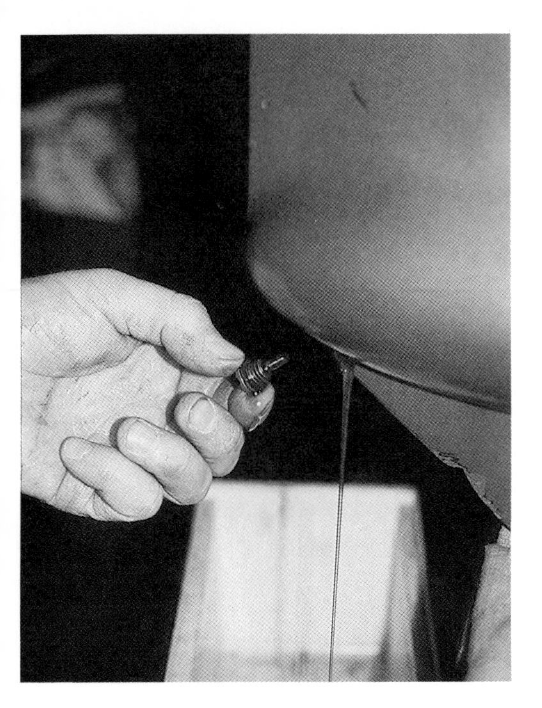

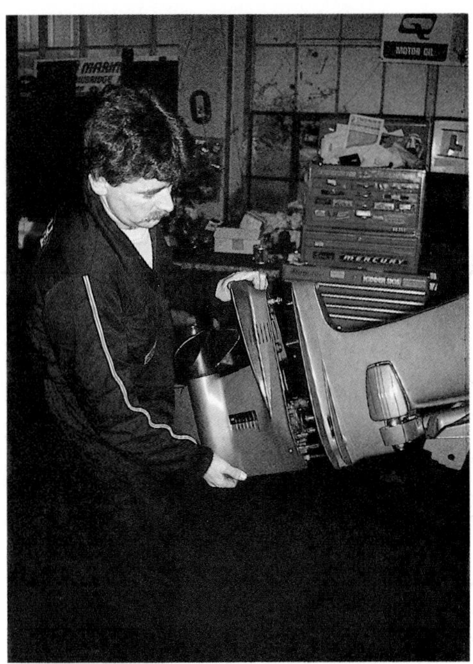

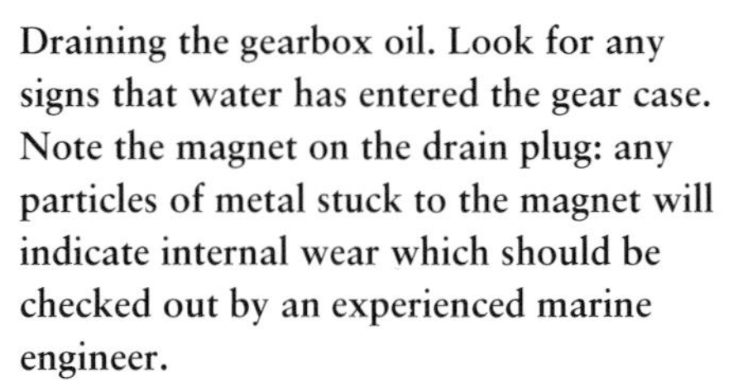
Draining the gearbox oil. Look for any signs that water has entered the gear case. Note the magnet on the drain plug: any particles of metal stuck to the magnet will indicate internal wear which should be checked out by an experienced marine engineer.

Replacing the lower engine leg. Renew all gaskets and grease all studs and bolts with a marine-grade grease.

If you see any metal on the magnet, there has been internal gearbox wear which will obviously have to be rectified. Ensure the rubber washers on both drain and vent plugs are in good order before refitting them. Only refill the gearbox with a quality marine lubricant as specified by the manufacturer.

Removing the propeller is the next step. Most manufacturers recommend the propeller is checked, removed and the spline regreased every six weeks. Examine the shear pin, fitted to the prop shaft, for distortion and replace with a new one if required. The shaft should then be cleaned and regreased to assist future dismantling. When refitting the propeller, ensure the securing nut is torqued to the manufacturer's recommendation, and the nut securing tabs are bent back to prevent the nut working loose.

Before refitting the gearbox, grease all studs, splines and bolts with a suitable lubricant. This prevents corrosion, and will also make life a lot easier the next time the box has to be removed. The gearbox is refitted in the reverse order of dismantling it, but the flywheel might have to be turned a bit to realign the shaft splines. Check that the gears are working before going on any further.

The engine's fuel filter should be replaced on an annual basis, or at more frequent intervals depending on use. On many modern engines these are a new for old part, on others only the insert is replaced. Obviously check connections for perishing or wear, not only on the filter but in the entire fuel system.

Always fit a new set of spark plugs having first checked the gap is set at the specified distance. Then spray the entire powerhead with a rust preventative spray. General lubricants like WD40 are OK, but they are not as effective in the long term as proper marine products, which offer greater protection from damp and corrosion. All that now remains to be done is to grease all grease nipples and check all steering components for slackness or wear, applying grease where required.

Having ensured everything is back together, run the engine either in a tank of water or with a proper adaptor over the cooling water inlet. Check the water pump is working correctly; a good stream of water should come out of the discharge port.

Now is also a good time to check the battery state and condition, cleaning any electrical connectors where necessary. Your engine is now ready for use again. Remember no matter how thorough the service, it will need another in a maximum of twelve months' time, even if it has little use in the mean time.

Preparing an engine for lay-up

Ideally, engines should be removed from the transom prior to a period of long-term stowage, unless the entire boat can be stored undercover. A combination of months of cold, damp and often bitterly icy weather can seriously damage an engine left out and exposed to the elements.

Be sure to remove every trace of salt water from the engine, both inside and out. Give the engine a thorough wash externally using hot soapy water (car 'wash 'n' wax' products are ideal), followed by a rinse off in clean, fresh water. Next, either by placing the engine in a water butt or by using an ear muff-type cooling water adaptor, you should run the engine for at least five minutes to

An 'ear muff' outboard engine cooling water adaptor in use. These are ideal for flushing the engine in fresh water after use, and to run the engine at regular intervals. Only run the engine at tick-over speed when using an adaptor.

thoroughly wash out all traces of salt.

It is important to wash the engine externally first so that any damp that gets around the powerhead will be dried off when the engine is run to flush it internally. Following this procedure, the engine should be allowed to stand for at least an hour to allow every trace of water to drain away. Water expands when it freezes, and even the smallest amount of water can expand enough to crack a major internal component.

While the engine is running, with the cooling water adaptor fitted, remove the cowling and locate the carburettor. Spray a storage fogging oil preparation into the carburettor inlet valve. Most big manufacturers now produce these excellent protective lubricants, which coat the inside of the cylinders and crank shaft very effectively with a protective coat of oil, minimizing any risk of corrosion during a period of inactivity. Be sure to read the instructions printed on the can before use and follow them to the letter.

With the engine still running, disconnect the fuel supply when you feel the engine has been flushed long enough, and allow it to run dry. Fuel allowed to remain inside the carburettor, fuel lines, cylinders, etc., will deteriorate and gel in time, and may condense and increase the chances of corrosion, almost certainly causing starting problems at the beginning of the next season.

It is worth noting that petrol stored for long periods inside petrol tanks and cans deteriorates in quality. One of the commonest reasons for engines not starting following a lay-up period is poor-quality fuel. Pour any excess petrol into your car fuel tank. It doesn't matter if the fuel has two-stroke oil mixed in as this will do your car no harm.

It is strongly recommended that the gearbox oil is changed prior to a lay-up. If any traces of water have entered the lower leg and caused the oil to begin to emulsify, corrosion is highly likely. Changing the gearbox oil frequently only takes a few minutes and only costs a few pounds. Be sure to check the integrity of all gaskets, replacing as necessary.

It is very important to remove the propeller and grease the spline every six weeks or so to prevent it seizing on to the shaft spline. Leaving the prop in position and ungreased throughout the winter is asking for trouble. Removing a prop takes just a few minutes, then all you need to do is clean and regrease the spline. Apply a liberal coating of a marine grease to the spline-locating grooves and the internal surface in the prop hub. I recommend you leave the prop removed until you next need to use the engine.

A lot of anglers totally forget to give the steering and throttle linkages a good clean and regrease. Tube-type steering systems in particular are very prone to seizing so it is imperative that they are frequently greased and moved backwards and forwards a few times to keep them running smoothly.

The last stage of the overwintering plan should be a good spray of WD40 or a marine equivalent over the entire powerhead, and every other accessible part of the engine. This cleans away any dirt or other residues, leaving behind a protective layer of oil that repels damp. Repeat this about once a month throughout the winter to help keep your engine in pristine condition.

The engine should now be in good shape to see the winter through, but a quick check every month will ensure it emerges on top form at the start of the new season. As mentioned above, frequent applications of WD40 will keep it clean and damp-free. Regularly working the steering and throttle linkages will prevent seizing. Turning the engine over slowly by hand, when this is possible, will ensure all internal components maintain a protective film of oil.

Trailer maintenance

The following advice is intended as a general guide to servicing trailers. None of the tasks detailed are beyond anyone with basic skills and require only a minimum of tools and a tub of quality marine grease.

The trailer wheel bearings, if they are allowed to seize, are invariably the biggest cause of problems associated with trailers. Keeping them in perfect working order is simplicity itself. Slacken the wheel nuts off slightly, while the weight of the boat and trailer are still on the wheel. Using an ordinary scissors-type car jack, jack up one of the wheels until it is just off the ground. Place a concrete block or blocks of wood under the axle to prevent the trailer falling in case the jack slips.

Remove the wheel, then the dust cap on the hub. Next, remove the split pin through the main axle shaft and the castellated nut which holds the bearings and the hub. Slide the entire hub off the axle, taking care not to lose the thrust washers located beneath the nut.

There are two types of bearings found on boat trailers. The most common are the taper roller bearings but quite a few trailers are fitted with ball-bearings, which are slightly more difficult to strip out, but do tend to be of a better quality than typical roller bearings.

If the bearings are stiff, seized or if there are any signs of rust, clean off as much old grease as you can with rags, and then soak the bearings in petrol or some other degreaser for about half an hour. This should clean out all traces of the old grease as well as any sand or grit. Dry the bearings thoroughly using clean rags, and examine them closely. If they are still stiff and feel rough when revolved, or if they are excessively slack, replace them. The old bearings are worth keeping for use in an emergency, depending on condition, but my advice would be to fit new bearings if you have the slightest doubt.

Reassembly of the hubs is easy. Smear a layer of grease on to the axle shaft to prevent the bearings sticking to it. Both bearings should be given a coating of grease, making certain as much grease as possible is worked in between the balls or rollers. The inner bearing, the one with the rubber seal, is then slid on to the shaft, followed by the hub, which should also be given a liberal but not excessive coating of grease on the inside edges where they make contact with the bearings.

Refit the outer bearing, followed by the thrust washer. The castellated nut should be tightened to a little more than finger pressure and the split pin refitted. It should now be possible to revolve the hub easily by hand, but without any lateral wobble. If there does appear to be excessive sideways play in the hub either slightly tighten the nut or try fitting a second thrust washer; or replace the bearings. On no account overtighten this nut as within a very short time the bearings will overheat and collapse.

Refitting the dust cap is next, followed by the wheel. Tighten the wheel nuts as much as you can with the wheel off the ground, tightening those opposite each other first to ensure even pressure is applied and that the wheel is fitted squarely on to the hub. Tighten the nuts further when the wheel is lowered off the jack, but make sure that you do not apply too much pressure as this will strain the hub studs or the wheel nuts.

Give the wheel a good spin before it is lowered off the jack to work the grease into all parts of the bearings, then test again for any excessive lateral play. If the wheel does wobble, restrip and start again. Normally, worn bearings are the cause but in some cases fitting a second thrust washer can help eliminate slack.

If the hubs are fitted with a grease nipple do not be tempted to do away with a frequent strip down in favour of pumping the hubs out with grease. The only way to ensure the hubs are in a good working order and properly lubricated is to strip them down and grease them by hand as detailed above.

If you have a trailer fitted with brakes, it is advisable to service the entire system. This is perhaps the one job best left to someone with mechanical skills, if you feel you do not want to attempt the job yourself. Provided you work in a methodical way, stripping and servicing a brake system is not too difficult but it is very important that the entire system is functioning correctly and not working on one side only.

Prevention is always better than cure. The best advice I can offer owners of braked trailers is wherever possible only submerge the minimum section of trailer into sea water. Hose the trailer off with fresh water as soon as possible. Frequent sprays with a release oil such as WD40 can also help to prevent parts seizing.

Trailer rollers must be well greased. If the rollers do not function properly then launching and retrieving the boat will cause the keel band to quickly cut flat spots into the rubber. This will exaggerate the situation by preventing the rollers from rolling, ultimately putting a lot of extra strain on the trailer winch and the boat bow eye.

Stripping the rollers down is very easy and is ideally a job to be carried out with the boat off the trailer. However, if this is not possible, careful jacking and manoeuvring of the hull should allow you access to the rollers.

Once stripped down, clean the roller shafts with fine wet and dry sandpaper, and clean out as much old grease from the centre of the roller as you can. Regrease the shaft and push it into the roller, making sure it can be rotated by hand. Once again only use a quality marine grease, which will remain effective for far longer than a general-purpose motor grease. If the rollers have developed flat spots they should be replaced.

The trailer winch should also be stripped down, cleaned and regreased at least once a year. Pay particular attention to the gearing teeth. If these have started to show signs of wear it is worthwhile considering replacing the winch. A winch with slipping gears is a real pain to use, especially on steep slips. Always make sure you fit a winch powerful enough for the combined load of the boat, engine, and all the equipment carried for a day's fishing. A more powerful winch will be easier to use than one used at its maximum rating and will last a lot longer.

Now is also a good time to inspect the winch cable. Steel wire is lethal as a winch cable, as it will snap without warning. Good-quality nylon rope is far better, and will last a lot longer. Another good choice is a length of nylon webbing strap.

All other moving parts of the trailer should be examined, cleaned and oiled or greased as applicable. These include the ball hitch coupling, the jockey wheel, any hull rollers, and the break-back hinge and pin, when fitted. Basically, if it is designed to move, you should periodically clean and grease it.

The final job is to check the tightness of all nuts and bolts holding the trailer frame together. Locking nuts should always be used but even these can work loose. It is also worth inspecting any welds for signs of corrosion or cracking. The trailer tyres should be kept at the same standard as the tyres on your car, including the spare which should always be carried. Any signs of corrosion on the trailer metalwork should be rubbed down, and then painted with a quality paint such as Hammerite.

I strongly advise that you give your trailer some form of security marking. Stamp, engrave, or even weld, your post code and as much other information as you can on to the trailer. Mark the largest component of the trailer, which is normally the main longitudinal section, or backbone. If you only mark a smaller component it will be an easy task for any thief simply to change that part. Also, it is a good idea to mark the trailer in a place where it is easily seen, as this can further deter any potential thief.

7 Dinghy-fishing techniques

In general, the techniques used by the dinghy angler will be the same as those used by an angler fishing aboard a larger charter boat. However, because of such factors as space and the flexibility to pick and choose marks and techniques at will throughout the day's fishing, the dinghy angler will often have far more scope for experimentation than his counterpart, fishing perhaps as one of up to 12 anglers aboard a charter boat.

Other techniques, such as trolling and the use of downriggers, are rarely practised or indeed possible aboard a crowded charter boat and in many situations only the dinghy angler can use them with any great success. Even when the more traditional approach such as uptide or downtide fishing are being used, the dinghy angler can reap several advantages over the charter angler. When foul weather keeps the charter fleet in port, the dinghy angler can often find a protected bay or headland and enjoy a full day's sport.

Two anglers fishing aboard a typical 16-ft dinghy can quite realistically fish two rods each uptide and a third downtide, with a minimal chance of tangling. On occasions, I have fished three rods uptide, and worked a float or a spinner on a fourth.

The advantages of fishing a multi-rod technique are many. If, for example, fish are thin on the ground, the more baits the angler has in the water the greater is the chance of success. But the real advantage so far as I am concerned is that several rods allow the use of several baits, which will both help to establish the most productive bait of the day and increase the variety of the day's catch by attracting different species.

Uptiding

Uptiding is generally accepted in many areas today as being one of the most productive methods of boat fishing. The reason why uptiding is so successful is two-fold. Firstly, baits that are fishing well away from the scare area caused by a boat anchored in shallow water, are more likely to be located by species of fish which have a tendency to swim away from noise disturbance. Secondly, when fishing in a strong tide, uptiding with a grip lead is the most efficient way of maintaining bottom contact when using light tackle.

The basic uptiding outfit will consist of a 9-ft to 10-ft rod which should possess the following characteristics: a sensitive tip for bite detection, a gutsy, yet forgiving, middle third to facilitate casting and handling sizeable fish in strong tides, and a powerful butt for additional inherent strength. Uptide rods are rated by the weight of lead they are intended to cast, usually 2–4 oz, 4–6 oz, or 6–8 oz. A rod

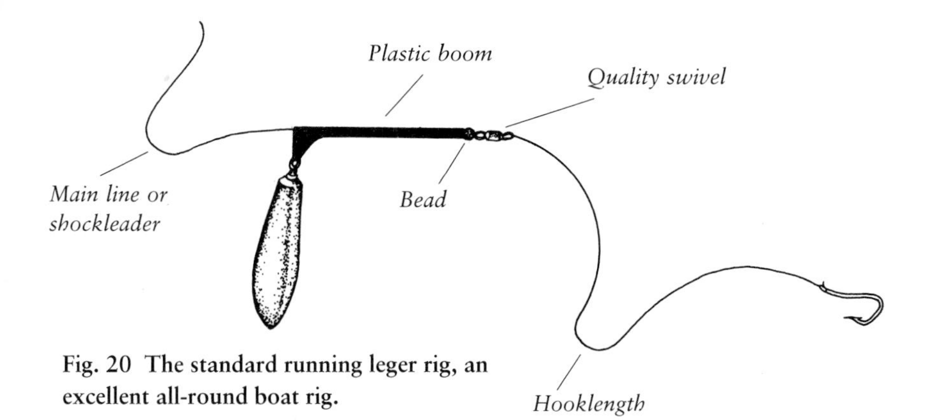

Fig. 20 The standard running leger rig, an excellent all-round boat rig.

capable of casting around 5 oz will be the most useful all-round rod. The rod should be matched with a quality reel, usually a multiplier; the ABU 7000 and Shimano Speedmaster are both excellent uptiding reels.

For the overwhelming majority of situations the simple running leger is the most efficient and productive end rig. Quite simply, a 4-in tubi-type boom is threaded on to the main line, followed by a small bead and a small, high-quality swivel. The hooklength is attached to the other end of the swivel. A 15-lb BS is probably the most widely used line for uptide fishing, though specific situations often call for lighter or heavier lines (Fig. 20).

Whether or not to use a 50-lb BS shockleader has been the subject of much debate. Personally, I almost always use a shockleader when uptiding. The use of a leader not only prevents irritating and often dangerous 'crack offs', but it can help to prevent fish losses. Due to the uptiding technique, a long length of line will be lying on or very near to the seabed (Fig. 21). When fishing over rough or hard ground there is a very real chance of this line getting damaged, and suddenly snapping when playing a decent fish. In addition, big fish can be extremely difficult to handle in a strong tide, and a leader will give the angler extra security when landing the fish.

The disadvantages of using a leader are, firstly, if it is not correctly tied, the joining knot can fail when playing a good fish and weed and other debris can collect around the knot and jam in the top rod ring, making it difficult to land a fish. The alternative is to use a heavier breaking strain of line on the reel, such as 25 lb BS.

Fig. 21 Angle of line when fishing uptide.

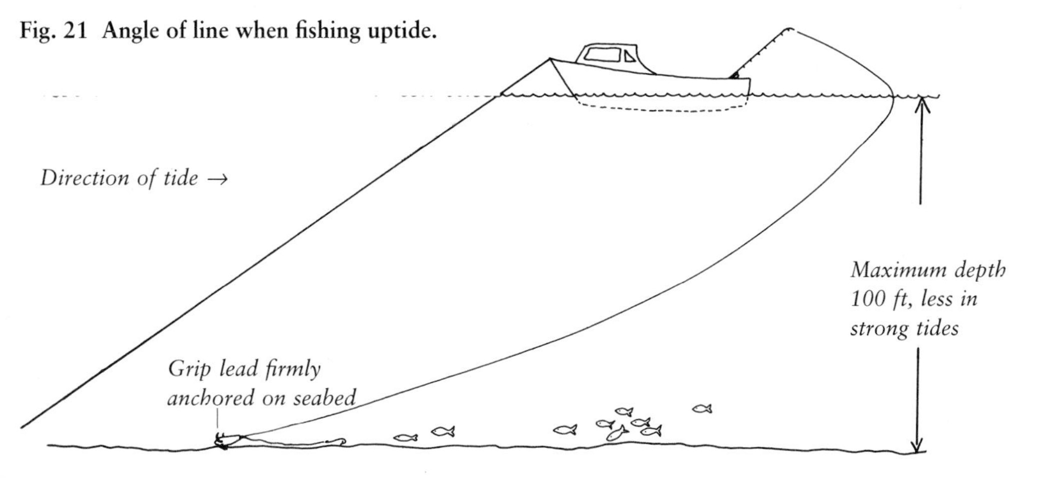

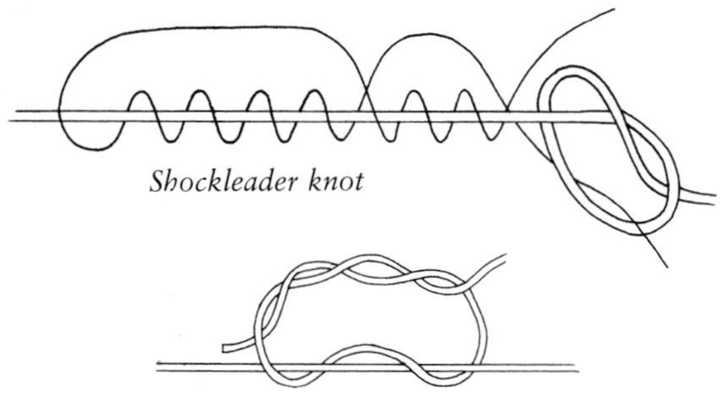

Shockleader knot

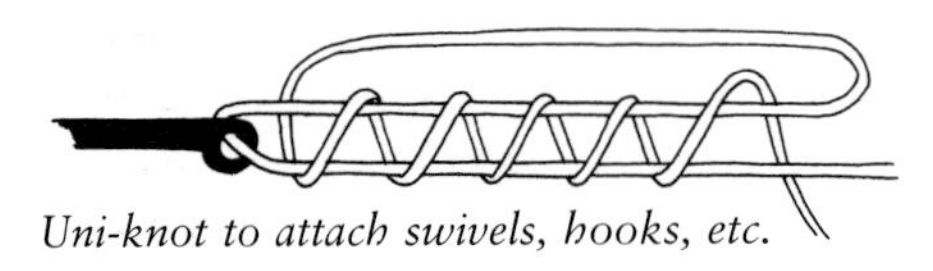

Stop knot used, for example, when float fishing

Uni-knot to attach swivels, hooks, etc.

Tucked half blood knot to attach swivels, hooks, etc.

Fig. 22 Selection of useful fishing knots.

The final choice will be down to the individual; it is advisable to brush up on your knot-tying techniques (Fig. 22).

Basic uptiding involves casting the baited end rig up and across the tide, approximately at an angle to the anchor warp of 45 degrees. This angle should be decreased when fishing in very strong tides to improve the lead's chances of gripping, and increased in slack tides or at high water. Following casting, the lead is allowed to fall swiftly and freely down to the bottom, then a bow of slack line is released in order to assist the lead gripping by reducing the angle between the reel line and the sea bed.

The rod should now be left in a secure rod rest, the tip bowing over in the tide. Bites will be indicated either by a delicate tapping on the rod tip, or as the classic uptide bite: the rod tip suddenly dips and then springs upright when a decent fish takes the bait and breaks the lead free as it swims off, usually hooking itself in the process. In either case the angler does not strike immediately, but quickly retrieves all slack line until in a straight line of contact with the fish. Only when the weight of the fish can be clearly felt should the angler attempt to set the hook with a single firm pull.

Casting up and across the tide using a plain lead and allowing the tide to slowly drag the terminal tackle across the sea bed can be deadly for the likes of flatfish and rays. A moving bait will be far more likely to locate individual fish.

Downtiding

For many years downtiding or up-and-down fishing was the standard way of fishing afloat. The angler drops his baited end rig over the side, lowers it down to the bottom and waits for a bite. But successful downtiding is a real art, and not as simple as you might at first think.

The essential skill when fishing downtide is in maintaining bottom contact, as most UK species of saltwater fish are bottom feeders. Unless a horrendous lump of lead is used, the tide will very quickly raise the terminal tackle well clear of the bottom and well out of reach of the fish.

The skilled downtide angler will hold the rod at all times, using just enough lead to maintain bottom contact. With the reel in free spool, slowly trot the bait back in the tide, occasionally slightly raising and lowering the rod tip and tapping the lead on the bottom, to confirm you are fishing at the correct depth (Fig. 23).

Bites are generally clearly felt, but the angler must resist the urge to strike pre-

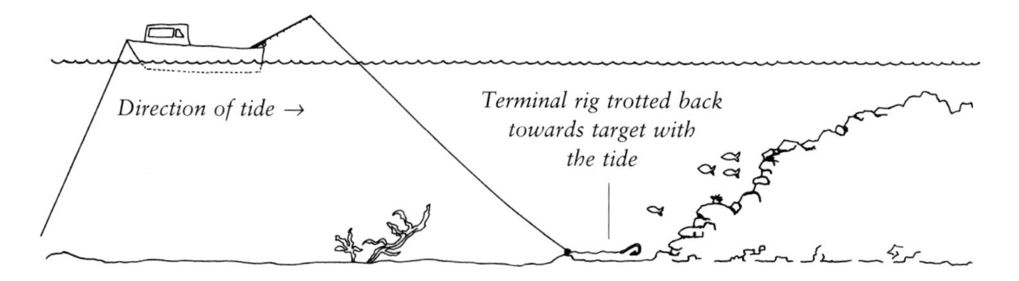

maturely. Instead the fish should be given a few yards of slack line and time to take the bait. Only then should the angler re-engage the reel spool and strike.

A typical downtide outfit will consist of a 6-ft to 7-ft rod, rated in line classes of either 6 lb, 12 lb, 20 lb, 30 lb, or 50 lb. The stated line class gives a very approximate indication of the breaking strain of line to be used. A 30-lb-class rod is a good all-rounder for fishing in the UK, although a 20-lb class or lighter will invariably offer far more sport. The good old running leger is once again the best general terminal rig.

Close in

Far too many dinghy anglers never give the slightest consideration to fishing within a mile of the shore, yet around some parts of our coast this will often be the best strategy. Totally featureless areas are few and far between, and the smallest reef or sandbank will attract fish. Any rock headland projecting into the tidal stream will create an area of disturbance known as a tide race, which will attract the likes of bass, pollack and mackerel, which gather to prey on small fish in the turbulent water.

There are other advantages to fishing marks which are very close to the shore. Get to know your local inshore ground well and often you will be able to get afloat and fish in perfect safety when bad weather conditions prevent fishing offshore. Headlands provide an excellent lee when the wind is in the right direction, often providing flat calm seas for several hundred yards.

Fig. 23 Method of downtide fishing a reef or wreck from a boat anchored uptide.

One of the nicest things I find about fishing these sort of marks is that you really don't know what you are going to catch. Fish an offshore sandbank and you can expect rays, flatfish along with bass or tope in some areas. Fish a wreck and you can expect a handful of other species. But fish an inshore reef and you never know what's going to take your bait next.

The variety of fish that inhabit inshore waters is staggering. From my own local area in the Bristol Channel alone I have personally recorded well in excess of 40 species, with one or two known to exist in the area yet to be caught. On the whole the more obscure species will be on the small side and include the likes of bream, gurnards, wrasse and mini-species, in addition to occasional exotics such as red mullet, trigger fish and John Dory, all of which increasingly figure in UK rod and line catches.

You should never allow yourself to become complacent when fishing for smaller fish. Over the years I have had several surprises when I have resigned myself to fishing for smaller fish. Bass and cod into double figures have appeared on

several occasions, along with tope, big eels and one or two which never made it to the boat.

Closely studying an Admiralty chart for your area will help to find likely inshore marks, but don't expect too much detailed information unless your area is near a commercial port and large-scale charts are available. General charts are excellent for offshore work, but the sort of marks I am referring to often lie within a couple of hundred yards from the shore.

A fishfinder will prove invaluable when examining an area in detail. Slowly running your boat across it in different directions with the bottom portion zoomed up on the screen will reveal a lot of detail. The real beauty with inshore marks is that once they have been located they are so close to the shore that by taking reference marks from the adjacent rocks, etc., they can be accurately logged and revisited without sophisticated navigation equipment.

In areas with a large tidal range, a walk at low water on spring-tides can reveal a lot of useful information. Many marks dry out at low water on these big tides and the amount of detail which can be gleaned is invaluable.

The sort of ground you should aim to find is a patch of sand amidst an expanse of rock, or perhaps an isolated outcrop of rock within an area of sand. Gullies are always excellent features for attracting fish, drawn to hunt the vast varieties of different items of food that gullies provide. Sand bars at the mouths of rivers attract many items of food such as sand-eels, which in turn attract fish. Mussel beds are often associated with local hot spots, notably for plaice and other flatfish. Even small areas of weed or pebbles on an otherwise open sandy beach will attract something at high water.

So, having decided on the area you would like to fish, how do you go about fishing it? Of course much will depend on what sort of area it is. You will have to consider such factors as water depth, the tidal state and strength, along with the time of the year. I often use two rods, one rigged with a single decent-sized bait, the other incorporating a two- or three-hook rig baited with a selection of different baits.

A pollack caught on an American soft rubber worm lure; these can be deadly when fished on light tackle.

Opposite **Fishing on the drift within 100 yds of a sheer cliff face. Often excellent fishing can be found within casting range of the shore.**

Typical baits I would use on the first rod are some form of fish, whole squid or peeler crab; livebaits are always worth trying. On the second rod small pieces of fish, crab or squid are also a good choice, but king rag, live prawns or any of the various types of shellfish should never be ignored.

A float is a good way to present a small bait on light tackle over an area of very rough ground and it will allow you to fish a much wider area than you could with a static bait. Floats really come into their own when fishing livebaits such as prawns, sandeels, ragworm and small fish, all of which can be presented in an irresistible way beneath a float.

Fig. 24 Simple yet effective rig for fishing either American soft rubber worm lures or live worms.

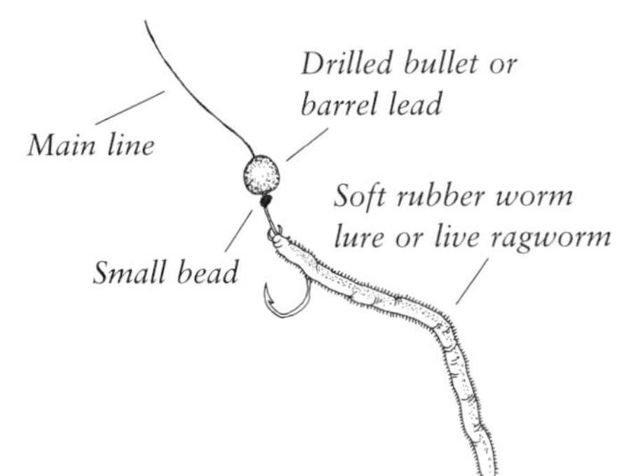

A lot of the better fish present over inshore marks will be predators and can be caught on an artificial lure. Most of the many traditional spinners and spoons will catch fish. On very light tackle, jigging American soft rubber worms can prove deadly (Fig 24). Over shallow reefs or rock outcrops, floating plugs catch a lot of fish, including bass, pollack and wrasse. Long slim jointed plugs are the best all-rounders. Trolling is another very effective method of working lures over inshore marks.

Fishing on the drift

Fishing aboard a drifting dinghy is a very efficient technique for presenting a bait or lure when attempting to cover as much ground as possible in order to locate isolated pockets of feeding fish. Over clean ground, drifting can look deceptively easy, but the angler's prime objective is to ensure his bait maintains contact with the bottom at all times. The vast majority of UK species are bottom feeders and baits allowed to trail in mid-water will catch few fish.

A simple running leger with hook lengths up to 6 ft (double or more when fishing for plaice) is the ideal end rig for fishing on the drift. A tube-type boom of about 4 in will help keep the rig tangle-free and assist bait presentation. A small bead protects the knot and a small, quality swivel completes the trace. The breaking strain of nylon used will depend on the target species. Consider 20-lb BS as being a minimum, but step up to 40 lb or 50 lb if you anticipate rays or big turbot.

You should aim to use just enough weight to keep the tackle on the seabed but not so much as to overload the rod. Old-fashioned circular studded watch

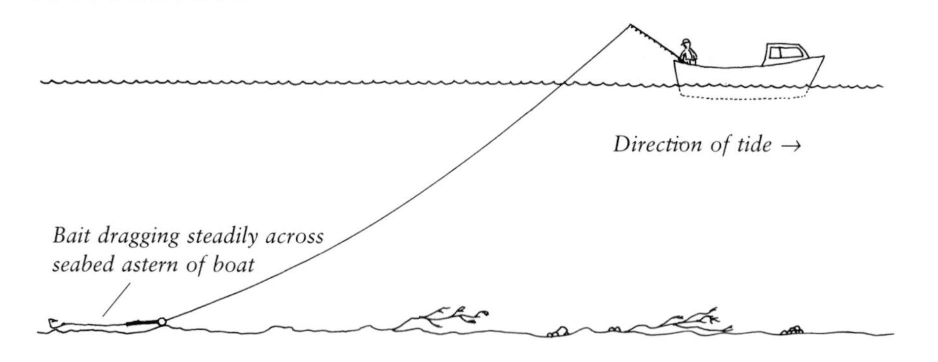

Fig. 25 Method of fishing on the drift over clean ground.

leads are ideal for drift fishing; they disturb the sand as they drag across the bottom and attract the fish. The addition of an attractor spoon on the hooklength, about 6 in from the baited hook, is popular when fishing for plaice and other flatfish, along with many other species.

The bait is always lowered over the side of the boat facing away from the direction of the drift, to avoid the line dragging back under the boat's keel. Let the bait fall to the bottom slowly or the hooklength will spin back around the main line.

When you feel the lead touch the bottom do not immediately re-engage the reel. Using your thumb, check the line running off the spool. A small multiplier is a far better choice than a fixed spool for drifting. Release a few more yards of line, then, with the spool checked, slightly raise the rod tip and lower it to confirm that the bait is still on the bottom. If not, release a little more line. This process is repeated throughout the drift, with the baited rig getting further and further behind the boat (Fig. 25).

If a bite is felt, resist the urge to strike and release a few more yards of line to avoid moving the baited hook away from the fish. After about a minute, check the line leaving the spool with your thumb; if the fish is still there you should feel a rattle on the rod tip, or the rod will slowly bend over against the resistance caused by the weight of the fish. Re-engage the spool, retrieve any slack, and with one steady movement raise the rod to set the hook.

Drifting over rough ground is far more difficult and in general the angler will require heavier tackle to cope with the rocky condition. A medium boat outfit will cope with the majority of conditions, but a heavier 50-lb class might well be required over the roughest marks, or in very deep water and strong tide situations which demand heavier leads.

The running leger rig is again the most efficient all-round rig, but a paternoster rig, with the baits above the weight, can be a better choice when fishing over the roughest ground. It is a good idea to fish the lead off a weak line, in order to limit tackle losses to just the lead. Shorter hook snoods will reduce snags (Fig. 26).

When drifting over rough ground avoid baits trailing behind the boat in the same way as when drifting over clean ground. This will prevent the end rig from getting dragged into snags. It is important to maintain as near a vertical line as possible between rod tip and end rig. In order to achieve this, an extra couple of ounces of lead may be required.

When fishing over broken ground such as reefs or wrecks, various types of lures can be very productive (Fig. 27). In general, it is possible to fish with far

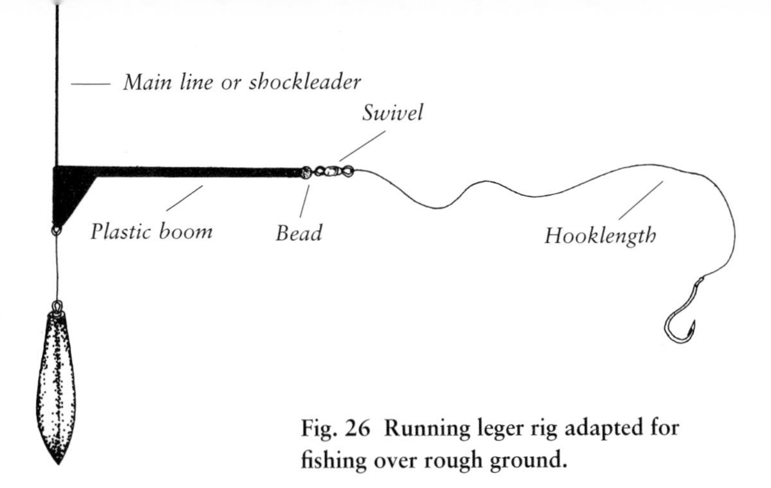

Fig. 26 Running leger rig adapted for fishing over rough ground.

lighter tackle when using lures over rough ground, than would be required when fishing baits.

Trolling

Trolling and the use of downriggers is widely practised in many countries around the world, and is steadily on the increase in the UK, especially among dinghy anglers. Trolling involves trailing artificial lures, and occasionally natural baits, at a distance behind a moving boat. The technique ensures that the lures cover a large area and can be useful when exploring new ground such as a reef. Target species include pollack, coalfish, bass, cod, mackerel and, on rare occasions, sea trout.

The simplest form of trolling involves tying the lure on to the end of the reel line, releasing about 50 yds of line, and slowly trolling it along. Almost any type of lure can be used, but diving plugs and artificial sandeels are particularly effective. The rod must be firmly held in a secure rod rest, so that if a fish takes or if the lure becomes snagged the extra weight coming suddenly on to the rod does not pull it overboard.

The above technique is known as flat-line trolling, and is suitable for depths up to about 30 ft. When trolling in deeper water, it is necessary to make the lure swim deeper to draw fish from cover. There are several ways to achieve this.

Fig. 27 Method of fishing on the drift with artificial lures.

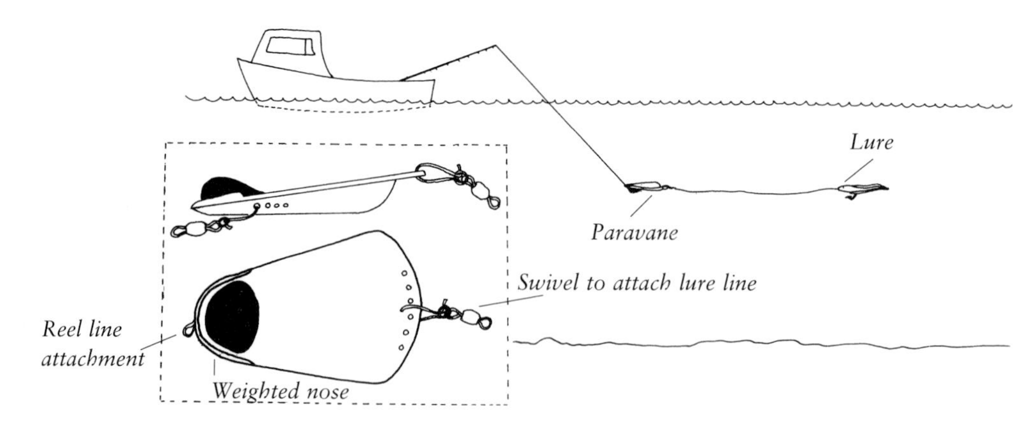

Fig. 28 Paravanes and their use in trolling.

The easiest method is to attach a heavy barrel lead or a purpose-designed trolling lead above the lure. The angler will now not only be playing the hooked fish but also the lead. Several designs of plug are available which dive extremely deep, and these, too, can be used to great effect.

Tackle shops often stock special diving vanes, known as paravanes. These are again attached at a distance above the lure, and are so designed to dive to a set depth, trailing the lure attached to a length of line behind them (Fig. 28).

None of the above methods allow the angler accurately to gauge the working depth of his lures and, when covering a rapidly alternating seabed, with pinnacles standing high in the water, lure losses are inevitable.

The answer is to use a downrigger. A

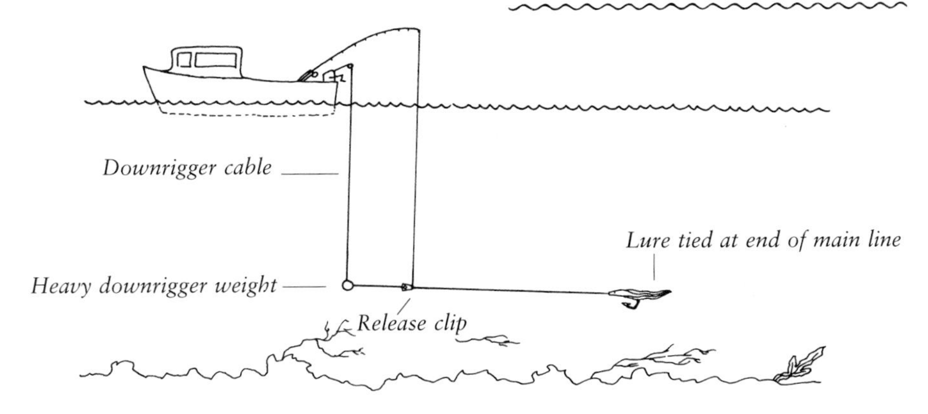

downrigger is a specialist piece of equipment that clamps or bolts securely on to the side of the boat. It consists of a drum of steel wire that threads through a short arm, then down to a heavy cannon ball-type weight. Attached to the weight is a short length of wire and a special release clip.

The rod is held in a rod rest, which normally forms part of the downrigger. With the lure attached, about 20 ft of line is released and allowed to straighten out behind the boat, which by now should be slowly making way through the water.

Then the line is clipped into the release clip and the cannon ball is steadily lowered, taking the release clip

Opposite **An angler clipping the reel line into the quick-release clip fitted to a downrigger. Downriggers open up many excellent opportunities for the dinghy**

Fig. 29 A downrigger in use.

and the lure with it. A counter on the downrigger allows the angler to set very accurately the depth at which the lure swims (Fig. 29).

By working in conjunction with a good fishfinder, it is possible to ensure that the lure swims extremely close to snags. Many fish will be lying there, yet there will be little fear of snagging. If the depth starts to shallow off, the angler simply raises the cannon ball accordingly.

When a fish strikes at the lure, there should be sufficient tension in the release clip to set the hook before the line snaps free. The angler can now enjoy playing his fish without the hindrance of any cumbersome terminal tackle. The downrigger should be wound in straight away to prevent the fish taking the reel line around the downrigger wire.

8 Fish species

Bass

Distribution

It used to be widely quoted that you could not catch bass north of a line drawn from Anglesey to the Wash. Today this is certainly not the case; I have personally caught several bass from beaches on the extreme northern tip of Scotland. That said, the bass still remains primarily a fish of the south and west of the country.

Fishing for bass

Bass can be caught using a wide range of techniques from uptiding to light tackle lure fishing. A true opportunist, the bass frequents an equally wide range of different habitats, ranging from tiny backwater creeks through to deep-water wrecks many miles offshore. The bass is an ideal target species for the dinghy angler, who, with his versatility and freedom of choice of techniques, is well equipped to pursue them.

In most parts of the country bass are inshore between approximately April and the end of November. During the year their diet ranges widely from chasing tiny fry and whitebait in mid-water well offshore, to foraging among the kelp beds for peeler crabs, often within a few feet of the shoreline. In order successfully to catch bass the dinghy angler must be quick to recognize these changes in lifestyle and diet, as often bass become totally preoccupied with just one food item to the exclusion of everything else.

Your approach should be first to locate an area where bass are present. Establish whether the fish are present all of the time or just for certain times of the day or tide. Then try to determine on what, and how, the fish are feeding, and match your approach accordingly. At all times you should exercise extreme stealth and caution; only then can you hope to succeed regularly with bass.

Cod

Distribution

Cod, by far the most popular species of salt-water fish in the British Isles, have a nationwide distribution and at some time of the year will be present inshore around all parts of the coastline. In the south of the country this is generally throughout the autumn and winter, though north of East Anglia and throughout Scotland cod remain inshore throughout the year.

Fishing for cod

Cod are very much a dinghy angler's species and the actual technique the angler adopts will usually be chosen to match the prevailing conditions. In shallow water areas such as the Thames Estuary and the Bristol Channel uptiding is invariably the most efficient method of catching cod.

Above left **A prime cod of around 9 lb, caught by Jonathan Delance uptiding in the Bristol Channel.**

Above right **Tony Kortens, sales manager for Orkney Boats, displays a specimen Irish pollack caught on light tackle off the Kerry coast in western Ireland.**

In deeper water more traditional methods take over, including fishing on the drift with all sorts of lures and pirking over reefs and wrecks.

Cod is another species which are caught on a wide range of baits. Various different types of marine worms top the list for codling but squid and large fish baits, including livebaits, are more effective for the bigger specimens.

Pollack and coalfish

Distribution

Both pollack and coalfish can be caught throughout the British Isles, but they are not common in the southern half of the North Sea. Many smaller specimens inhabit inshore reefs and wrecks along with an occasional bigger fish. The best specimens are invariably taken well offshore in deeper water, either over reefs or, more usually, wrecks.

Fishing for pollack and coalfish

The normal method for catching pollack and coalfish offshore is by using some sort of artificial lure, notably rubber sandeels, fished off a flying collar rig. American-style soft rubber worm baits are also increasing in popularity. Live ragworms, lightly hooked through the head and fished off a long flowing trace, are another and often deadly bait for catching these fish. But perhaps the most effective is a live sandeel. Live sandeels can now be readily obtained through tackle shops throughout the summer, and whenever possible the dinghy angler should equip the boat with the necessary livebait tanks to exploit this most deadly bait to the full.

Tope

Distribution

Tope have a fairly widespread national distribution but those areas where they are regularly caught by anglers tend to be localized. The most productive areas include the Thames Estuary, the Nab Tower area of the eastern Solent, the Bristol Channel, West Wales, the Lancashire coast of the Irish Sea and one or two of the sea lochs off the west coast of Scotland.

Tope are usually inshore within angling range between the months of May and September.

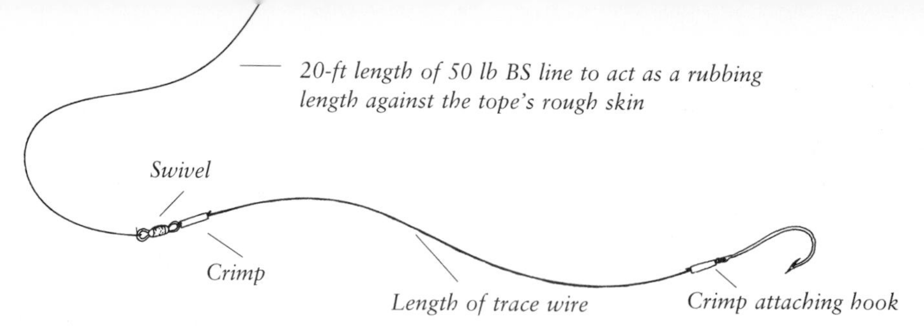

Fig. 30 Standard wire trace used for tope, conger and shark.

Fishing for tope

Many of the areas where tope are caught are extremely shallow. Therefore uptiding is by far the most sporting method for catching this hard-fighting species of fish. Tope baits are usually various types of fish, especially mackerel and herring, but in some areas, such as the Isle of Man, sandeels are often used to great effect. In recent years, sections of silver eel have become popular among tope specialists and have accounted for numerous specimen fish, including the current record fish.

Tope are members of the shark family, and have a vicious set of very sharp teeth. As a result it is always necessary to use a short length of suitable wire to prevent bite offs, along with approximately 20 ft of heavy mono, about 50 lb BS, to prevent the main line becoming damaged from contact with the tope's rough skin (Fig. 30).

Plaice, dabs and flounders

Distribution

Plaice, dabs and flounders have always been popular with dinghy anglers, because, among other reasons, they can be caught well inshore and on light tackle. All three have a national distribution and, whereas flounders show a high tolerance of fresh and brackish water, plaice and dabs are far more at home in pure, undiluted salt water.

Fishing for plaice, dabs and flounders

Obviously, with three species of fish with average weights of less than 2 lb, it is essential to use tackle that is as light as possible to get any sport out of catching them. Wherever possible, tackle of no heavier than 12-lb class boat gear, a light uptider or even spinning tackle should be used. Occasionally heavier outfits will be required to cope with the prevailing conditions, but not the fish. Fishing on the drift is standard practice amongst flattie specialists, but fishing at anchor and allowing baits to trot back and roll around in the tide is also productive.

All three species can be caught on a wide selection of baits, including various types of marine worms, shellfish, fish, and peeler crabs. Dabs show a distinct preference for fish baits, even if they are seemingly well past their best. Plaice can often be tempted on a cocktail of three or more different baits. Many top specialists rate peeler crab as the number one bait for flounders.

If there is one common denominator in catching these three species, it has to be an interest in various types of artificial attractors, including spoons, beads and sequins. These are often used by anglers targeting flatfish in the belief that the fish are drawn by different colours and vibrations. Whether or not this is the case, enough specimen flatties have been caught over the years by anglers using artificial attractors in conjunction with natural baits. I for one will continue using them.

The author with a nice plaice. Note the coloured beads on the hooklength, often used for additional attraction when targeting flatfish.

Safely in the net! A spotted ray.

Rays

Distribution

There are four common species of ray in British waters: the thornback, the small-eyed, the spotted and the blonde ray. Stingrays are occasionally caught in some areas, but their distribution is extremely localized. The thornback ray has the widest distribution and can be caught more or less anywhere. The other three remain predominantly species of the south and west of the country.

Fishing for rays

More often than not the tactics the dinghy angler adopts when targeting rays will be dictated by the fishing conditions and not the fish themselves. Wherever possible, uptiding will provide the most sport, but in deep water and fast tides the angler will probably have to revert back to standard downtiding techniques.

In general, rays are caught over open ground. Small-eyed rays in particular favour systems of sand and shingle banks, often in very shallow water. Thornback

Chris Martin displays a double-figure small-eyed ray, caught from a sandbank in the Bristol Channel.

rays are also caught over similar ground, but venture further into brackish water associated with estuaries. They often favour areas of mud, especially in the vicinity of mussel beds. Spotted rays are often caught over rough ground, but more often than not from flatter ground or areas of sand and gravel. Blonde rays show a distinct preference for deep water gullies, especially fast tides running across sandbanks.

Various types of fish bait are the best all-round choice for rays, and generally the fresher the better. The number one bait for small-eyed rays is sandeel and, funnily enough, previously frozen eels often outfish fresh ones when fishing for rays. Peeler crabs, various marine worms and shellfish are other useful baits. Wire hooklengths are not necessary when ray fishing as the fish do not have sharp teeth. However, a heavy mono trace tied from approximately 50 lb BS is advisable, along with a strong hook, as rays have powerful jaws.

Conger eels

Distribution

The conger eel is one of the most powerful fish the dinghy angler can ever realistically expect to encounter. Conger are widely distributed along the southern and western coastlines of the British Isles, and although a few are undoubtedly present in the North Sea, they are rarely taken on rod and line. The vast majority of conger that are caught come from wrecks, especially the bigger specimens: most inshore reefs are populated by conger, albeit of a smaller average size.

Fishing for conger eels

Conger have little tolerance of cold water and migrate offshore into deeper water during the coldest months. The best time to catch them is from about May through to the autumn, when they feed heavily prior to the winter.

Powerful fish demand powerful tackle and when fishing for conger strong tackle is needed, not only to handle the fish, but initially to drag it clear of its lair. Even a modest eel would be difficult to move if it was allowed to get its tail wrapped around a rock or the ironwork of a wreck. The minimum gear recommended for conger fishing is 30 lb class.

The conger is a true predator, hence fresh fish, notably mackerel and pouting, invariably make the most effective baits. Cuttlefish is also used with a great deal of success by some conger specialists. Either wire or heavy-duty nylon of around 200 lb BS is essential for use as hooklengths.

Aboard a small dinghy even a strap conger of about 20 lb can be a real handful, and unhooking the fish outboard can save a lot of hassle and mess. Night fishing is often far more productive than daytime fishing, especially when fishing over either the high or low slack water periods.

Wrasse

Distribution

Wrasse are widely distributed around the British Isles and it is only the southern half of the North Sea where they are not found. Wrasse favour deep, clear water and show little tolerance of brackish water, hence their scarcity in this area and a few other areas such as the upper reaches of the Bristol Channel.

Fishing for wrasse

The ideal way to fish for wrasse aboard a dinghy is by steadily drifting over an inshore reef. Often the very biggest wrasse are caught right at the water's edge, especially where sheer cliffs drop into deep water. Wrasse are occasionally caught on artificial lures, such as mackerel feathers or Hockeye lures, but natural baits are far more productive.

Mel Russ, editor of *Sea Angler* magazine and his girlfriend Tina with two beautiful wrasse. The fish were caught at Brandon on the west coast of Ireland; note how far from the rocks they were fishing.

Right **Kevin Launder holds a double-figure common smooth hound, taken uptiding in very shallow water.**

Crab is unquestionably the number one bait for wrasse. I prefer peeler crab, but many specialists only ever use hard backs in the belief that they sort out the better-quality fish. This may well be so, but by using hard backs you are really limiting yourself to catching just wrasse. Peeler crab is a far more effective all-round bait and more likely to tempt a bonus fish such as a bass, cod or bream. Live ragworm, lugworm and most types of shellfish also work well.

Wrasse are an extremely hard-fighting fish and strong tackle is often needed to prevent them diving back into cover. For maximum light tackle sport, floatfishing for wrasse takes a lot of beating.

By using a float, it is often possible to tempt a wrasse to leave its sanctuary amidst the rock and kelp and rise into clear water to take a bait; then all you have to do is stop it crash diving back into cover! Summer and autumn are usually the most productive seasons to fish for wrasse.

Smooth hounds

Distribution

Smooth hounds probably have a much wider distribution than is generally realized. The best-known smooth-hound hotspots are the Thames Estuary, the Solent and the Bristol Channel. A few fish are taken off the Cornish coast, and from West and North Wales, but, by and large, these tend to be infrequent catches of small fish.

Fishing for smooth hounds

Most of the established smooth-hound areas listed above occur in relatively shallow water with a strong run of tide. Hence uptiding is by far the most successful method of catching this hard-fighting sport fish. An average smooth hound, from most areas, probably weighs in excess of 10 lb. Pound for pound I would suggest the smooth hound is at least twice as powerful as a tope. This is surprising as crab is the staple diet of the smooth hound, and it hardly take tremendous reserves of speed and energy to hunt for crabs.

Naturally, therefore, crab is the number one bait for smooth hounds. Again, peeler crabs are my own preference as they appeal not only to hounds but to many other species. Hermit crabs are also used to great effect in many areas, as are hard-back crabs, but I have found a peeler crab takes a lot of beating. Ragworm, squid and occasionally fish will also tempt smooth hounds.

Smooth hounds do not have sharp teeth; instead they have powerful flat jaws, similar to a ray, designed for crushing crabs. Mono of about 50 lb BS is perfectly adequate for use as a hook-length. When hooked, smooth hounds often take off on long, powerful runs, especially in shallow water. A reel with a smooth and correctly set clutch is an absolute must. In most areas the smooth hound season starts at the end of May and lasts until September.

Black bream

Distribution

Bream is another species with an extremely localized distribution. In those areas where they do occur, fishing from a dinghy is often the most efficient way of catching them. The Sussex, Hampshire and Dorset coastlines are the main bream areas but they are also caught in many areas of Wales.

Fishing for black bream

Black bream are found on reefs, wrecks and, occasionally, in more open conditions, especially in the vicinity of mussel beds. Those marks, where they are caught, tend to be very localized and often it is necessary to position the boat to within a few yards for maximum success. Groundbait is widely used amongst bream anglers.

The most productive bream baits are long thin strips of squid and fish, all types of marine worms and shellfish, and small chunks of peeler crabs. Cocktail baits can be particularly effective for bream, as can the addition of coloured beads and sequins on the hooklength.

Many bream marks are located really close to the shoreline and often in very shallow water. The ideal way to fish for bream is to anchor the boat just up-tide of the reef or wreck which is holding the fish, then slowly trot the bait down-tide towards the fish. Black bream are extremely powerful little fish and put up a tremendous fight on light tackle. The first fish appear inshore in May, and they will often remain until the autumn.

Turbot and brill

Distribution

In general turbot and brill are widely distributed around the British Isles but those areas where they are regularly caught tend to be localized. The main areas for catching both species are often associated with systems of sandbanks and fast tides, such as the prolific Shambles Bank off the Dorset coast, and Skerries Bank and Lanacombe Bay off South Devon. More turbot are caught in the countless systems of banks found in the Bristol Channel than anywhere else, but these are small fish that rarely exceed 5 lb.

Fishing for turbot and brill

The classic way to fish for turbot and brill is on the drift. Given an extensive system of banks, drifting is by far the most successful way for locating any isolated pockets of fish or even a lone fish. Both the turbot and brill are voracious predators but they tend to lie in wait for their prey on the downtide side of a bank or in gullies, rather than actively searching for food. On an isolated bank or gulley, it might be more practical to fish from an anchored boat positioned just uptide of the feature and trot baits downtide towards the fish. Alternatively, it is often possible to cast up and across the tide, using plain leads light enough for the tide to roll them across the bottom, dragging the bait towards the fish.

A big turbot can top 20 lb and is a very powerful fish. If you are specifically targeting big turbot, which is more or less impossible today, you should use either 20 lb or 30 lb class gear or a medium uptide rod. For more moderate fish, lighter tackle will provide more sport. Both species are usually inshore within fishing range between April and the autumn.

Sharks

Distribution

Of the four species of shark caught around the British Isles, only the blue shark is a realistic proposition for the dinghy angler. Porbeagle sharks tend to average in excess of 100 lb and are extremely powerful fish, which are potentially very dangerous in the confines of a small boat. Thresher sharks, too, should be avoided unless you have a lot of experience. The mako shark is rarely seen but best avoided in small boats.

Blue sharks are a warm-water species, caught during the summer months off the south west of Devon, Cornwall and Ireland. With an average size of around 50 lb or 60 lb, these make great light tackle opponents in small boats, weather permitting.

Fishing for shark

The standard way of fishing for sharks is drifting. The use of rubby dubby is essential for success and the anglers should make every effort to set up as long a scent trail as possible. Minced mackerel, mixed with bran and liberal additions of fish oil, is the usual rubby dubby. The art is to attract the shark without feeding them on chunks of thickly cut fish.

I would not advise any inexperienced angler to use less than 30 lb class gear for sharks, at least until he or she has taken a few. A strong wire trace and 12 ft rubbing length of heavy mono is essential. Only use bronzed hooks which can be cut off and left to rust away inside the fish when, as frequently happens, the shark ends up deeply hooked. It is good practice to release most fish outboard in the water, not only from a personal safety point of view but to minimize any risk of damage to the fish.

Conversion table

1 in = 2.5 cm
1 ft = 30.4 cm
1 yd = 0.9 metre
1 mile = 1.6 km
1 oz = 28.3 g
1 lb = 0.4 kg
1 ton = 1.016 tonnes
$°F = \frac{9 \times °C}{5} + 32$

Index

Page numbers in **bold** refer to the illustrations